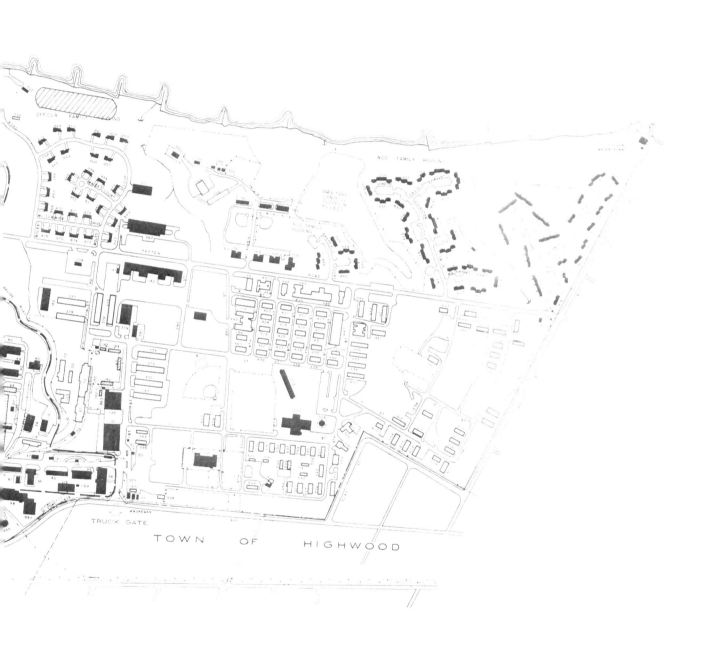

TOWN OF HIGHWOOD

VIEW FROM THE TOWER

A HISTORY OF FORT SHERIDAN, ILLINOIS

by

Martha E. Sorenson

and

Douglas A. Martz,

Major, United States Army

Cover Design: "Tower Print"

©Copyright, 1978

Officers' Wives Club, Fort Sheridan, Illinois

Inquiries may be directed to:

Tower Enterprises
P.O. Box 103
Highwood, Illinois 60040

TABLE OF CONTENTS

PART I

PART II

FOREWARD

Fort Sheridan, Illinois, is a geographically small Army post, unpretentious by most standards and located twenty-five miles north of Chicago. Even though it did not play a part in any of the Indian Wars, it sits astride what was once a major movement area for aboriginal Indians. Yet there has been a sequence of people and events that have contributed to the special uniqueness of Fort Sheridan.

For millions of men and women, Fort Sheridan was either the beginning or the end of their military service. For some who remember the Great Depression, Fort Sheridan was a training center where shelter, food and self-confidence were earned in equal amounts. For still others, Fort Sheridan was a place where soldiers lived, trained and worked; and where the dashing young Cavalry officers caused many hearts to flutter.

Today Fort Sheridan is still a deceptively quiet post, pastoral in its appearance, but underneath it is a beehive of intense and directed activity. It is a post that is dedicated to its soldiers, those whose memory it preserves and those who serve or will serve in and around its enclosure.

Fort Sheridan is a historic post. Its architecture and design are unique among Army installations. Its buildings have earned a place in the National Register of Historic Places, and just recently the entire installation became a National Landmark. A cohesiveness of purpose, unity of construction and functional arrangement contribute to Fort Sheridan's inherent pride — what it contributes to the Army that built it and what it gives to the communities by which it is surrounded. The American history which Fort Sheridan has helped forge and the physical history of its buildings have caused this account to be written. We who have researched and recorded it have lived within its boundaries. We have been influenced by its rich and textured past, its present and the promise of its future.

It is impossible to name all the people who have helped present this history. However, we are indebted to former Post Commander, Colonel George Marko (United States Army, retired) and Colonel Stanley Thomas, United States Army, Post Commander, for allowing us access to Fort Sheridan's offices and records. Without their cooperation this book could not have been written.

Other special people who contributed freely of their time, information and encouragement are: George Argianas (Fort Sheridan), Bruno Bertucci (Highland Park), George Campbell (Wilmette), Alice Conway (Lake Forest), Susan Dart (Lake Forest), Dawn Frevert (Arlington Heights), Bill Goodall (Highwood), John A. Holabird, Jr., FAIA (Holabird and Root), Arthur Johnson (Commercial Club, Chicago), Thomas G. Kocher (Curator, Fort Sheridan Museum), Eric Lundahl (Fort Sheridan), Mrs. Barrett K. Mason (Highland Park), Frank Nustra (Highwood), Frank Phillips (Highwood), Patricia Reeves (Fort Sheridan), Peter Rettig (Highwood), Robbie Robinson (Highland Park Historical Society), Nina Smith (former Curator, Fort Sheridan Museum), Kaye Tocci (Fort Sheridan), Karl E. Wiegand (Elmwood Park).

At the beginning and at the ending, too, there are our spouses. They have done more than simply endure the time we spent researching our facts and reading our drafts. They have encouraged us to tell our post's history that others may learn it as we have. More importantly, without the soldiers who have served, who now serve, and who will serve in the future at Fort Sheridan, this book could not have been written. It is to them this work is dedicated.

Fort Sheridan, Illinois
April, 1986

Part One

THE FORMATIVE YEARS

The Great Glacier came out of the North and enveloped most of the State of Illinois. It pushed southward, shoving, scraping and accumulating debris in its path. The warmer climate melted its face, but it stayed awhile, perhaps hundreds of years. The Glacier continued to pile up further debris from the retreat and advancement of the ice sheets that brought more ice. There was a gradual warming trend and further melting. Eventually the Great Glacier was forced to retreat permanently, but not without surrendering its burden and forming a moraine.

Fort Sheridan is located on the Highland Park glacial moraine, also known as the Valparaiso glacial moraine. The area is very fertile and well-watered, drained by six streams flowing eastward through deep ravines into Lake Michigan, creating bluffs, cliffs and natural canyons, some of which have greatly eroded.[1] The areas surrounding Fort Sheridan are abundant with flora, fauna and legend. The area was reputed to be part of Paul Bunyan's logging territory, while the Great Lakes were reportedly formed by a fall taken by the Great Blue Ox, Babe. The truth has more to do with winds, waves and glaciers than with ox, timber and lumberjacks. Many factors of land formation, disintegration and alteration have been at work in the past to produce the present features of this region. Most of them are still hard at work.[2]

Chicago's storm winds, the same winds giving the Windy City its nickname, generally come from the Northwest, piling up waves that crumble the shores and heap the sand upon the beaches.[3] The surface features of this area are due chiefly to the glacial deposits of the Wisconsin Period, the last glacial period that enveloped part of North America approximately eleven thousand years ago.[4] The deposits it left produced flat and fertile prairies and were the natural earth movers forming the Great Lakes. Part of the Lake Michigan bluff at Fort Sheridan contains the only remaining example of open prairie-like vegetation that once was a major natural feature in Illinois. The Illinois Department of Conservation has determined its fragile ecology is of statewide significance and has defined protected sites for the threatened and endangered species of plants.[5]

Green Bay, Wisconsin, had been established as a French trading post and mission about 1670 and was the oldest settlement in the Northern Territory. It is certain present-day Fort Sheridan was on an Indian trail between this and other French trading posts in Wisconsin and their hunting grounds and villages in and around Chicago. The tribes headed north on the Green Bay Trail originating at what is now Diversey Street in Chicago. The trail proceeded along North Clark Street, generally staying near the lake shore, veered east of Rose Hill Cemetery, skirted ravines to Highwood and continued north across the post's rifle range.[6] As far as can be determined, all the Indians that have occupied Lake County as their home were of the Algonquin family and almost exclusively the tribes of the Illinois and the Potawatomi.[7] The Chicago portage was a popular rendezvous, and the Illinois Indians were so identified with this locality that Lake Michigan was generally known to early explorers as the "Lake of the Illinois," the original name of Lake Michigan.[8]

The Potawatomi, the last major tribe that made its habitat in the Chicago area, were called Prairie Indians and lived mostly on wild fowl, fish and buffalo. Eventually white men found their way into the area and concluded a series of treaties with the Indians. Like most of these treaties, they were largely unfair and widely ignored by the whites who made them. The last Indian treaty in Illinois was negotiated at Chicago, September 26,

1833. In that treaty, the Potawatomi ceded to the United States all that remained of their land in Illinois, including Lake County, Deerfield Township.[9] As the treaties were concluded and both trade and travel expanded between Chicago and Wisconsin, the Green Bay Trail became a thoroughfare and was also known as the Military Road from the days of Fort Dearborn (established in 1803 and located at Michigan Avenue and Wacker Drive, Chicago) when military troops provided safe passage for pioneers trekking to Green Bay. Later, when foot and horse stepped aside for coaches, stagecoach passengers had a rough trip enroute when the weather was less than fair.

According to local lore, third-class passengers had to push the coach when its wheels sank in the mud; second-class fares were asked to lighten the load by walking; and first-class passengers were respectfully requested to sit still.[10] Another story that circulated during this period involved a traveler who had been discovered in a notorious Chicago mudhole, buried right up to his neck. "Don't worry," he was reputed to have told alarmed bystanders. "I'm riding a horse."[11]

Travel continued to increase, and the Military Road became the major highway between Chicago and Green Bay, Wisconsin. By common consent, the Military Road became known as Green Bay Road, a name it holds to the present time. Settlers followed travelers along Green Bay Road and bought what farm land they could afford. The earliest settlers in what is now Lake County could purchase land from the Government Land Office for $1.25 per acre. They were mostly a tidy lot generally hailing from New England where Horace Greeley's injunction to "Go West, Young Man" included the frontier region of Chicago. These hardy folk were predominately Irish, German and Scandinavian immigrants. They banded together for protection and farmed the land they had purchased, but refused to relinquish their individuality. After a good harvest, the farmers carried the fruits of their labor to the Chicago market by ox-drawn carts, a trip requiring approximately two to three days. Money was scarcer than hen's teeth according to local accounts, and debts were often paid in harvest, produce and staples. The main barter was flour, pork and eggs. Those who produced them were generally self-sufficient and very self-reliant. For example, the coffee the settlers made included parched corn, rye and barley. This concoction was mixed with coffee essence bought at the Chicago market.[12] Meat included buffalo and venison, which was supplemented by wild fowl and berries.

"But it was the climate that the early settler gloried the most. All the ills that flesh was heir to fell from the sufferer as soon as he breathed the life-giving healing breezes of the prairie."[13]

"Canyons at Fort Sheridan," from a post card postmarked 1833. *Highland Park Historical Society.*

2

Frank and Bridgit Gilgare on their farm, which was located between the golf club house and Wherry housing on Nicholson Road. *Highland Park Historical Society.*

The land immediately bordering the lake which later became Fort Sheridan had the lake on one side and deep ravines crossing it which, from the farmer's point of view, rendered the land mostly valueless.[14] The generally flat and fertile prairie to the west was valued for its productivity and was more often selected by the settlers for their farmland.

As a footnote to history, it is interesting that both Chicago and Fort Sheridan might have been southern parts of the State of Wisconsin. The original northern boundary of Illinois was once several miles south of its present location. It was the determination of Nathaniel Pope, Territorial Delegate to Congress in 1817, that kept Chicago and Fort Sheridan in Illinois. He foresaw the commercial possibilities of territory bordering the Great Lakes which housed a natural harbor (Calumet Lake) and could serve as a major transportation hub, not only by water but rail as well. He also felt that unless Illinois were given a northern water outlet (i.e. Lake Michigan) it would, in effect, become a southern state.[15]

In 1844 two enterprising men had the ambitious idea of using the lake and its natural shoreline to develop a shipping village to rival their neighbor to the north, Little Fort (now the City of Waukegan). John Hettinger and John Peterman bought land now encompassing part of the southeast portion of the post for $123.00 and called their enterprise St. Johns. The two men convinced the government to establish a post office and opened

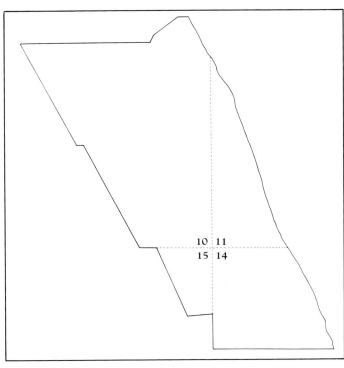

Outline of Fort Sheridan indicating Section 14. According to the plat on page 4, the Town of St. Johns occupied the north half of Section 14. (Township 43, Range 12) *Real Property Office, Fort Sheridan*

Clerk and Recorder's Office, Lake County, Waukegan, Illinois.

their doors for business. Their brick and lumber industries prospered until lake and weather asserted themselves, sinking a few of their lake vessels. Winter weather was not the only adversary. The civic morale was further undermined by continual wrangling over property rights and the founders' unsound policy of accepting land payments on the installment plan. If this were not enough, many of the townspeople were lured away by rumors of gold found in far off California.[16] St. Johns slowly melted away, except for the brickyard and rail spur, a speculative addition for later.

4

By 1869 Chicago had become a mecca for pioneers from the East and a gateway to their exploration of the West. Chicago was also home to the pioneers' main protection, the Division of the Missouri, quartered in Chicago and commanded by Lieutenant General Philip H. Sheridan. General Sheridan's responsibility was to maintain law and order in the frontier regions, which was most of the land lying west of Chicago. (The Headquarters, located at Washington and LaSalle Streets, was destroyed in the Chicago Fire).

Immigrants continued to come from their ancestral homes to a world that was no less hard and no less ready to thwart a man and cast him out. But this land, his new home, had a difference. It gave him something in return, more than the Old World could give, not simply in land but in dignity and personal freedom. This was the American Dream.

History records one such pioneer. Early in 1864 he bought a small, shingled cottage with a cow barn at the rear of the lot. It cost $500.00 and was located at 137 De Koven Street, Chicago. He and his wife worked hard, bought some livestock and hoped for a small profit. By 1871, Mr. and Mrs. Patrick O'Leary, by contemporary accounts, had become solid citizens among approximately 335,000 Chicagoans. On October 8 of that year they became legend. Despite accounts to the contrary, available evidence does not support the story that their cow kicked over a lantern, starting the Great Chicago Fire.

However the fire started, the result was the same — devastation of a hitherto unimagined scale. Chicago was a shambles. Only the two water towers and four buildings remained intact within a three and one third square mile area. Hundreds of people were dead, thousands were homeless. Looting and pillaging followed the fire, adding tinder to a combustible situation. The town fathers were panicked. They had never encountered such widespread devastation. Their training simply did not extend to housing and feeding thousands of homeless people on short notice with winter approaching.

The Mayor of the city, Roswell B. Mason, declared martial law and turned the city over to General Sheridan. General Sheridan accepted the responsibility and, with the approval of Secretary of War, W. W. Belknap, immediately requested companies of infantry from the frontier. He went further to organize help for the city by turning over blankets to the Chicago Relief and Aide Society, setting up tents for the homeless, and distributing rations to the needy.[17] One incident in particular best sums up his directness in dealing with the chaotic situation:

ORIGIN OF THE GREAT

FROM ORIGINAL

inline to Act of Congress in the year 1871 by H M kinsley in the office of the Librarian of Congress at Washington

O FIRE OCT.R 8th 1871.

.V. H. CROSBY.

Chicago Historical Society, ICHi-02945.

A certain hotel which had escaped the flames was reported as charging the exorbitant rate of $6.00 per day. "How much before the fire?" the General asked. The answer was $2.50. "All right," was Sheridan's reply, "I'll run this hotel myself for $2.50 a day." He put an orderly in charge and kept it full until martial law was removed.[18]

Governor John M. Palmer was offended that he was not consulted before martial law was put into effect. Palmer alleged the Mayor should have called on the state militia to preserve order and further protested Sheridan had violated the constitutional rights of Illinois by ordering troops into action. Nevertheless, Mayor Mason placed his trust in Sheridan who maintained order until martial law was removed on October 23.[19] This was the first, and hopefully the last, time that martial law was declared in the City of Chicago.

In 1883 General Sheridan was reassigned to the War Department in Washington, D.C. Upon his departure, Mr. John A. Doane of the Commercial Club of Chicago eulogized the departing hero:

"Chicago can never forget General Sheridan. When the city was in flames, when men's hearts failed them, and ruin and desolation stared us in the face, all eyes were turned to him . . . Believe me, General, a grateful people will embalm your memory in their innermost hearts . . . Your constant loyalty to this, your chosen city, a loyalty which its citizens can never forget so long as Chicago holds her proud place among the chief cities of the Union."[20]

**One dark night, — when people were in bed,
Old Mrs. Leary lit a lantern in her shed;
The cow kicked it over, winked its eye, and said,
There'll be a hot time in the old town tonight.**

quoted in the CHICAGO EVENING POST
and appears in THE GREAT CHICAGO FIRE
by Robert Cromie.
Author anonymous.

Waterworks after the fire of 1871.   *Chicago Historical Society, ICHi-13918.*

Water Tower, Chicago Avenue, 1890.   *Chicago Historical Society, ICHi-05902.*

THE GENESIS OF FORT SHERIDAN

Industrial turmoil between labor and management raged violently during the latter part of the nineteenth century in Chicago and elsewhere around the nation.

Early Chicago industrialists, Cyrus McCormick, George M. Pullman, Potter Palmer and Marshall Field knew that Socialists were preaching an entirely different doctrine to the so-called "wage classes." "Most numerous among the skilled and intelligent Germans, these agitators worked at trades by day and edited seditious pamphlets in dusty little printing shops at night. Pinkerton kept the big men informed of what the little men were up to, and the reports grew so alarming that Palmer and the rest raised a fund and started negotiations with the government at Washington for the establishment of Fort Sheridan and the Great Lakes Naval Station. The men in the counting houses felt safer with the Army and Navy close at hand."[21]

There were intensified efforts to organize labor unions. Chicago became a maelstrom of discontent as a result of the 1877 railway strike that began in the East and spread to Chicago. The discontent reached a climax in 1886 at Haymarket Square in Chicago where members of a labor party were peaceably assembled and noisily airing their grievances at a rally. (Haymarket Square was located at Randolph and Halsted and opened in the early 1850's. As residents moved away from the west side, the market became a place dealing in animal feed; hence the name "Haymarket Square").[22]

A local policeman demanded the meeting disband and threatened to use force if necessary. The crowd murmured its disapproval and the meeting disintegrated into warring factions. Someone threw a bomb into the crowd killing several people and injuring others. Riots ensued in the city streets.

"But every one who had lived through the desperate days after the fire of 1871 when the Federal troops kept the peace, or had seen the effect on the mob of 1877 of the mere arrival of those lean and dusty and Gatling-gunned veterans who made an object lesson march from the Union Depot to their camp on the Lake Front, will remember how he breathed more quietly when he knew that Uncle Sam was 'on deck' and the regulars 'at the bat.' "[23]

Chicago businessmen became increasingly convinced that Federal troops stationed near the city were a permanent necessity to cope with the turbulence and unrest generated by its workers. One man in particular was Senator C. B. Farwell. He was a member of the Commercial Club of Chicago, a group of conscientious businessmen who influenced Chicago's well-being, as they saw it. Senator Farwell had witnessed first-hand soldiers dealing with the Haymarket Riot when he returned to Chicago from a hunting trip on the same train bringing them from Fort Laramie, Wyoming.[24] The impression stayed with him, an impression he shared with his influential friends. Collectively, these businessmen decided to do something to get permanent troops into the area.

According to the minutes of the Commercial Club, a meeting was held May 30, 1885. The topic of conversation was a suitable location for an "artillery school" and "military station" near Chicago. A year later Marshall Field addressed the Commercial Club to formalize plans for a military installation. General Sheridan, also a member, was present and expressed his favorable opinion. This meeting was the conception of Fort Sheridan.

The Commercial Club acted decisively and in June of 1886 appointed three of its members (John A. Doane, C. B. Farwell and Alexander P. McClurg) to petition Secretary of War William C. Endicott for acceptance, by the United States Government, of a tract of land in the vicinity of Chicago for a military installation. The War Department found their logic impeccable and in the same month dispatched a team of Army officers to select such a site. The delegation included General Sheridan.

On July 2, 1886 the board of Army officers reported that a certain tract of land, designated as the Highwood Tract, possessed the greatest advantages of all the sites and recommended it to the Secretary of War.[25] The Highwood Tract was subsequently secured by the Commercial Club and donated to the government, a donation which was accepted by joint Congressional resolution dated March 3, 1887. The deed was signed October 6, 1887, and a copy hangs in the Fort Sheridan Museum.

Legally, the Commercial Club could neither own nor donate real property; so a Commercial Club consortium of Adolphus C. Bartlett, Charles L. Hutchinson, and John J. Janes acted as intermediaries. They and their wives are the grantors named in the deed. Two parcels of land were recorded on the same day. One parcel consisted of 598.5 acres and the other consisted of 34 acres. It was rumored that the additional 34 acres was donated with the understanding that the land would be used for military purposes or otherwise returned to heirs.[26] However, no limitations are set forth in the deed, nor is the Commercial Club of Chicago mentioned.

The realty consideration amounted to $10.00. It would be safe to speculate that the captains of industry in Chicago made generous contributions to enable the representatives of the Commercial Club to purchase the tract. The former owners included J. S. Prall, realtor, and Mr. and Mrs. Frank Gilgare.

"LITTLE PHIL" —
HERO AND BENEFACTOR

The post's "firsts" begin with the official creation of the fort itself. Lieutenant General Philip Henry Sheridan, in his capacity as the Commander-in-Chief of the Army, had Fort Sheridan signed into existence in 1888, and in so doing became the first living general officer to have a post named in his honor.

GENERAL ORDERS, HEADQUARTERS OF THE ARMY,
        ADJUTANT GENERAL'S OFFICE,
No. 11.   Washington, February 27, 1888.

The following order has been received from the War Department:

WAR DEPARTMENT, Washington, February 27, 1888.
By direction of the President the new military post at Highwood, near Chicago, Illinois, now called Camp at Highwood, will hereafter be known and designated as "Fort Sheridan," in honor of Lieutenant General Philip Henry Sheridan, U. S. Army.
WM. C. ENDICOTT,
Secretary of War

BY COMMAND OF LIEUTENANT GENERAL SHERIDAN:

R. C. DRUM,
Adjutant General.

OFFICIAL:

Assistant Adjutant General.

General Sheridan was as unique as the post which bears his name. He was born on March 6, 1831, the third of six children. Although no record of his birth can be found, his relatives admit he was born on the ocean when his parents came from Ireland to the New World. The "Biographical Register of the Officers and Graduates of the United States Military Academy" accept Albany, New York, as his birth place. His family did not settle long in Albany before they made Somerset, Ohio their permanent home.

Philip Sheridan's early ambitions for a military career began when he was appointed to the Military Academy at West Point, New York, in 1848. However, he was an unusual looking man whose physique was so peculiar that he came very close to being rejected by the examining board: He was barely 5'5" tall, barrel-chested, and his arms so long that his hands reached below his knees.

This was not a particularly happy time for Sheridan, academically or socially. His studies were a struggle, and he had the social stigma of being a Northerner and an Irish Catholic. At that time, the Academy was dominated professionally and socially by Southerners of the Episcopalian faith. Additionally, the influx of Irishmen to the United States during the famine (1848-1849) caused many Americans to become alarmed at the thought of a political imbalance and therefore ostracized them.

He was a plucky, fighting Irishman whose impetuous temper got him into trouble during his third year and he was recycled one year. In fact, Sheridan had gone over the limit for demerits at the time of graduation, but the Academy authorities gave him a reprieve believing his aggressive nature would be well channelled on the frontier. He received his commission as a Brevet Second Lieutenant of Infantry in 1853 and sent to the First Infantry Regiment at Fort Duncan, Texas. He remained there until 1855.

At the outbreak of the War Between the States, Sheridan was assigned to the St. Louis headquarters of the Armies of the Tennessee, Ohio and the Mississippi as a staff officer and Chief Quartermaster. However, he wanted a combat assignment and willingly resigned his Regular Army commission as Captain to become Colonel, United States Volunteers, commanding the Second Michigan Cavalry. In those days it was up to the governor of each state to appoint such officers. The governor of his home state of Ohio rejected the recommendation, whereas the governor of the State of Michigan appointed him. Sheridan became a Major General, United States Volunteers, in 1863 and a Major General in the Regular Army in 1864. President Abraham Lincoln, endorsing his Regular Army commission, confessed that he had always thought "a Cavalryman should be about 6'4", but 5'4" seems about right." (President Lincoln was a bit wary about praising his generals; hence he reduced Sheridan's height by one inch).

Of all the military men who rose from obscurity during the War Between the States, none traveled so far and so fast as Little Phil. His eulogized ride to the battlefield at Cedar Creek, Virginia, made the general's horse, Rienzi, (also known as Winchester) almost as famous as his rider. It was at Rienzi, Mississippi, that he was presented the three-year old gelding of Black Hawk blood, regarded as vicious and unmanageable.

Besides his celebrated successful offensives during the War Between the States, Sheridan gained additional renown as an Indian fighter. He fought the Indians who marauded the white settlers; he also fought against the white men's encroachment of Indian lands. No well-defined policy had been laid down by the government for the discipline and control of Indians placed on reservations. Sheridan tried vainly to recommend enactments to not only protect the Indians from injustices but also to deal with their misdeeds, with the laws to be executed at the Indian agencies by authorized courts. However, Congress simply voted meager annuities, leaving the solution of the problem of Indian civilization to time and circumstance.

In 1869 General Sheridan was assigned to the Division of the Missouri and had his headquarters in Chicago. He was comfortable in Chicago and became active in its social affairs. He was an honorary member of all the Chicago clubs and was the first president of the Washington Park Club. He was also one of the investors in forming a professional baseball team, the Chicago White Stockings.[27] He had not settled down long before he received orders making him Special Commissioner of the United States to observe military operations in the war between France and Prussia. He was a guest of Chancellor Bismarck and witnessed the surrender of Napoleon III. He returned to Chicago from his European sojourn in 1871. On June 3, 1875, Lieutenant General Sheridan married Irene Rucker, daughter of General Daniel H. Rucker, retired Quartermaster General of the Army. They remained in Chicago until his transfer to Washington, D.C., in 1883.

By this time Sheridan had received the nation's highest military office — Commanding General, United States Army. He and his family resided in "Washington House," purchased for him by Chicago admirers. The Sheridans remained in Washington until July, 1888, when the family retired to Nonquit, Massachusetts. The Congress of the United States revived the active grade of General Officer, and Philip Sheridan received the honor of General, United States Army, sixty-six days before his death.

General Sheridan deserves considerable credit for helping to keep the Army receptive to new theories and techniques of warfare. He insisted that his officers look to the future and the inevitable changes. For this purpose he established the first postgraduate military institution in American history, now known as the Command and General Staff College, Fort Leavenworth, Kansas.

General Sheridan visited Fort Sheridan on May 5, 1888, and received his last review of troops. He died on August 5, 1888, Nonquit, Massachusetts, and is buried at Arlington National Cemetery, Virginia.[28]

Other Army posts have borne his name but have since been abandoned: Fort Sheridan, Colorado, renamed Fort Logan; and Camp Sheridan, Wyoming, renamed Fort Yellowstone.[29] One of General Sheridan's more peaceful pursuits was campaigning for the establishment of Yellowstone National Park, which once encompassed Fort Yellowstone.[30]

"Sheridan's Ride"   *Fort Sheridan Museum*

THE CAMP AT HIGHWOOD

Geographically, Fort Sheridan's 694.5 acres are located on the Lake Michigan lake front, between the communities of Lake Forest to the North, Highland Park to the South, and Highwood to the West. The post lies to the East of United States Highway 41, one of today's main roadways between Chicago and points north. In recent years the total acreage has been reduced by cession to Highwood, Lake Forest and Highland Park.

Even though the land bordering the lake was considered of little or no value to some of the farmers in the area, the Commercial Club and the board of reviewing officers had enough foresight to select the 632½ acres for its excellent possibilities. There was an abundance of natural materials for the construction of buildings and roadways. Superior sand and gravel could be taken from Lake Michigan in unlimited quantities; and clay suitable for manufacturing brick was also available in quantity, on site and from the local area. From a practical standpoint, it was an excellent site for an Army installation, with transportation by rail to the West and by the lake to the East. From an aesthetic standpoint, the acreage was a superb site. There was abundant natural beauty, trees and vegetation. The only detractor was ravines cutting through the post boundaries. The ravines were taken into account and their value to infantry and cavalry training emphasized. Three major ravines were later named in honor of the Commercial Club members who were instrumental in donating the land: Janes, Hutchinson and Bartlett.

The young encampment at Highwood, still only a plot of land and an idea, was renamed Fort Sheridan by direction of President Grover Cleveland on February 27, 1888. The post, however, prefers to celebrate its birthday on November 8, 1887, when Companies F and K of the Sixth Infantry Regiment arrived by rail at Highwood, Illinois, from Fort Douglas, Utah. Their arrival made Fort Sheridan a reality. Companies F and K boasted a combined strength of eighty soldiers commanded by Major William J. Lyster. The soldiers consisted of 5 officers, 10 sergeants, 8 corporals, 2 musicians, and 55 privates with 3 attached hospital corps personnel. According to the diary of one of the soldiers, there was an imminent need for their presence because eight anarchists were to be hung on November 11, and Chicago thought it would be safer to have a force of the Regulars present.[31]

Major Lyster soon realized that whatever accommodation was to be made for his troops had to be carved out of an untamed woodland. Upon his arrival, there was very little cleared area and a great deal of primeval undergrowth. The first provision was setting up tents: the officers had framed and floored tents and the enlisted men had conical-walled tents without flooring and with 5 men assigned to a tent. The tents were heated by Sibley stoves using wood and coal. Eventually Major Lyster exceeded his authorized allowance in order to keep his men from freezing and replaced most of the wood-burning stoves with coal-burning models for better utilization of heat. His ingenuity, however, backfired when he learned that Fort Sheridan had been budgeted four hundred cords of wood for the following winter — for his coal-burning models. He explained at some length in several letters to his headquarters that wood simply would not generate enough heat, particularly since the new wooden barracks had shrunk as the timber dried and formed cracks.

It is in the course of this series of letters that Lyster later desperately referred to Fort Sheridan as "this bleak situation" and finally relented and ordered wood stoves on the order of the Chief Quartermaster. The "bleak situation" was further magnified in trying to clothe and feed the soldiers adequately. The assistant surgeon found the clothing issued to the troops of good quality but not enough protection against the severe winter. He recommended the issue of buffalo coats, which unfortunately had long since been dropped from Quartermaster inventory. Major Lyster felt the "quality of food furnished is insufficient. Neither of the companies has vegetables, and the company funds are so small, and vegetables so high in this market that men are deprived of this necessary form of food." Furthermore, water from two mineral springs on the camp grounds was unsuitable for drinking, so water was provided from an artesian well one mile away in Highland Park and distributed daily from a water wagon.[32]

The "red tape" and other obstacles Major Lyster encountered in trying to provide the basic amenities for his troops would have overwhelmed a lesser man. It was through his patience and perseverance that Fort Sheridan slowly took shape; and by the time he terminated his command on September 2, 1890, the construction of permanent buildings was already underway.

In 1889 Congress appropriated $300,000.00 for permanent buildings on Fort Sheridan. These buildings would accommodate six companies of Infantry and four troops of Cavalry. The appropriation also included the water tower, a wharf, cemetery, and rifle range. Most of the brick laying was done that winter. Water was pumped from the lake and hauled to the construction site by horse-drawn tankers. The Chicago and Northwestern spur track (which still crosses Sheridan Road and terminates behind the Fort Sheridan Museum) was used to haul construction material to the post. Transporting the material from the spur to the construction site through the mud was extremely difficult.

Foremen and superintendents made their rounds on horseback to escape the churned up mire, only to sink up to their boot tops when they had to dismount. Old records also indicate that building supplies were hauled to the construction site a mile away through thick underbrush and mud.[33] It is believed that these supplies were brick and manufactured at the brickworks formerly owned and operated by the Village of St. Johns.

As noted on the map on page 12, there was an Arcadian Spring House, located in the ravine behind what is now the Community Club (Building 31). At one time, it is said, hotels or a health resort were planned to take advantage of the natural phenomenon. At another time certain real estate speculators planned to make the area surrounding Fort Sheridan a summer haven for the wealthy families of Chicago. The panic of 1873 forced these plans to be rearranged significantly and later caused them to be abandoned.[34] (The panic of 1873 was precipitated by the failure of Jay Cooke and Company, a banking house involved in financing the Northern Pacific Railroad. Over 5,000 business failed in the depression that followed).

A hospital was located on Walker Avenue in Highwood, just south of the installation. It was a private residence which apparently had been leased by the government as a temporary hospital until the Post Hospital could be constructed. An early Surgeon General's report indicated the wooden structure had any number of highly unsanitary conditions, making it totally unacceptable. The report undoubtedly hastened the construction of the permanent hospital. The map also notes a flagpole and temporary quarters on the west side of the southernmost ravine. These quarters lived up to their name and have long since been removed without a trace.

Life was tough; but, as Senator Farwell had noted, these were "Regulars." They persevered, and the post slowly took shape through the guidance of soldiers and civilians working side by side. The soldiers, though, were lucky. When they stopped working for the day they had a local place to sleep, first their tents and then wooden structures. Brick layers, hod carriers and carpenters were not quite as fortunate and sometimes had miles to travel before they reached their shelter. Gradually, some of the civilian workers began moving to Highwood.

Map showing
U.S. Military Reservation and Fort Sheridan.
between Highwood and Lake Forest
Lake County, Ill.
1888.

Scale 1 inch = 2,000 feet.

A. Fort Sheridan Line
B. Walker Street
C 1. Ravine No. 1
C 2.   "   " 2
C 3.   "   " 3
C 4.   "   " 4
C 5.   "   " 5
C 6.   "   " 6
D. Gurley farmhouse.
E. Pond.
F. Railroad cut.
G. Brickworks.
H. Boathouse.
I. Hospital.
K. Arcadian Spring house
— — — Boundary of the U.S. Military Reservation
L. Sweeny's crossing

Real Property Office, Fort Sheridan.

12

THE VILLAGE OF FORT SHERIDAN
AND FORT SHERIDAN PARK:
HIGHWOOD, ILLINOIS

The Village of Highwood was platted in 1868 and attracted immigrants who wished to purchase fertile farm land in the "high wood" north of Chicago and those who sought employment after the Chicago Fire evicted them from their homes. In time, the village became so identified with the new post that the name was changed to the Village of Fort Sheridan, eight months after the arrival of Major Lyster and his troops.

"Old Post," an area between Washington and Crofton Avenues, was part of Highwood. Shannon's Store, now a Schwinn bicycle shop on the corner of Washington Avenue and Sheridan Road, was the focal point of the area and had the first telephone installed in Highwood. Many residents of "Old Post" worked on the installation and were inducted into the various wars. Some are buried in the Post Cemetery. Their descendents still have fond memories of "Old Post" being a children's paradise: tobogganing down the hill by the Post Hospital (Bradley Loop), climbing the stairs of the water tower and fishing off the wharf.

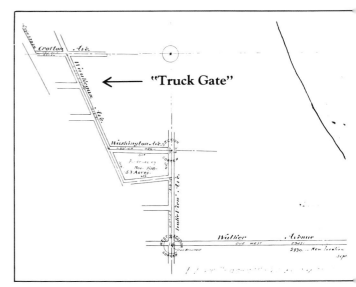

Real Property Office, Fort Sheridan.

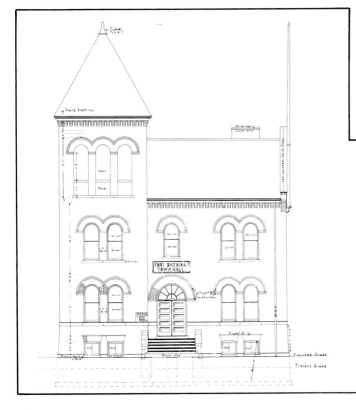

FRONT ELEVATION, WEST.
    Scale, 1/4 Inch = 1 Foot.

TOWN HALL AND JAIL

FOR THE TOWN OF

FORT SHERIDAN, ILLS.

H.D. GRODAVENT, ARCHITECT.
July, 1897.

Fort Sheridan Town Hall and jail, also known as the Fort Sheridan Village Hall. *City of Highwood.*

Top Row: Chas. Ackerman, Andrew Roeberg, Jim Duffy, Paul Pflagher, Ray Peterson, Arvid Roeberg, Hugh
Peterson, Clarence Monahan, Leo Carlson, Richard Laurentz, Ed. Brown, Albin Roeberg.
Center Row: Capt. Roger Moore, Fritz Walkter, Gust Ostrand, Matt Nugent, Frank Weinacht, Pat Hickey, John
Sheridan, John Peterson, Scotty Morren, John Hickey, Al. Huestis, Jim Watson, Ed. Mathews, Ed. Spellman.
Bottom Row: W.M. Wagner, John Nugent, Richard O'Conner, Harry Brownlee, Major Goheringer, W. F. Hogan
(Mayor), John Condon, Herman Swansan, Jake Fredine, James Reilley
Floyd Peterson

Volunteer Fire Department and city officials pictured in front of the Fort Sheridan Village Hall, circa 1906.
Apparently early plans for a military installation did not go unnoticed in Highwood. The stone commemorating this
building is dated 1886, a year before Major Lyster arrived, the year of the Haymarket Riot, and the same year Marshall
Field addressed the Commercial Club.

Highwood Fire Department

The only vestige of "Old Post" are the five homes still standing at the south end of the post. These homes were built by civilians and purchased by the government. Three of the houses were purchased in 1907, and the remaining two were acquired in 1908. According to local residents, Mr. Fink, the Wagonmaster, lived in one of them and Postmaster Sweeney lived in another. Other homes on what was "Old Post" were moved to Highwood when the land was purchased by the government in 1908, and some of these are still standing.[35]

The citizens of Highwood had mixed feelings about being a "garrison town." Some believed the village would become a "den of iniquity." Others saw increased profits and prosperity and welcomed the soldiers into their village.

"Dram" shops (saloons) became available to accommodate the influx of construction workers and soldiers to the area. Their presence posed such a problem to the local residents that it became necessary to ban the sale of liquor. Regardless, "blind

Building 111, located on D Street.
Reproduced from the original photograph by Nancy Powell, Fort Sheridan.

Building 113, located on D Street.　　*Reproduced from the original photograph by Nancy Powell, Fort Sheridan.*　　**Building 114, located on D Street.**

pigs" (places where liquor was sold in violation of law) flourished. Finally, it was decided that a liquor license of $1,000.00 would end the illegal trade with the stipulation that saloon keepers were forbidden to sell liquor to "lunatics, idiots, insane persons, minors, and habitual drunkards." Also, government authorities declared the Highwood Quadrangle off limits, thereby banning the sale of liquor within a boundary of one and one-eighth of a mile radius from the post. (The Highwood Quadrangle was the area on the United States Survey map from Lake Forest to the Cook County line).

There continued a mounting battle between the Law and Order League of Highwood (a group of Christian and civic-minded individuals who supported the anti-whiskey crusade) and saloon keepers. Finally, all saloons were closed in 1908 and remained so until state laws were enacted.[36]

The combined confrontations between the Law and Order League, the village trustees and the saloon keepers did not

dissuade the citizens from voting a city form of government in December, 1902. The City of Fort Sheridan remained so until October, 1904, and has since been known as the City of Highwood.[37]

In 1898 the Chicago and Milwaukee Electric Railroad constructed Fort Sheridan Park between Washington and Clay Avenues in Highwood. The park was to provide a "high-grade place of public entertainment" for the North Shore residents. Fort Sheridan Park boasted a dance hall, beer garden and theater. According to local accounts the park had a thriving summertime clientele from its opening July, 1898, until it was destroyed by fire in September, 1908. The government purchased this 5.3 acre parcel of land in November, 1910.

The Chicago and Milwaukee Electric Railroad tracks, parallelling what was then Waukegan Avenue and the Chicago and Northwestern tracks, ran from the park along the west side of the Post Stockade (now the Fort Sheridan Museum), across the western edge of the parade ground and up to the "North Gate." The line exited the property opposite Old Elm Road on its journey from Evanston to Waukegan.[38]

J. S. Prall, a local real estate developer and speculator, proposed building a "Fort Sheridan Subdivision."[39] The plans were stillborn because the government purchased this parcel in 1908. The proposed subdivision once had a ball park and greenhouse which have since disappeared. These various acquisitions added a total of 96½ acres to Fort Sheridan between 1906 and 1910.

Reproduced from the original photograph by Nancy Powell, Fort Sheridan.

Aerial view of Fort Sheridan and Highwood from Lawrence Captive Airship, 1908.
Reproduced from the original photograph by Herring, Highland Park.

Aerial view of Fort Sheridan and Highwood. The Chicago North Shore and Milwaukee Railroad Highwood yard can be seen in the foreground. Circa 1910. This area is now occupied by a motel and an apartment complex.
George Campbell, Wilmette

Fort Sheridan Park pavillion and Wells Ravine.   *Marvyn Wittelle, Highland Park.*

George Campbell, Wilmette

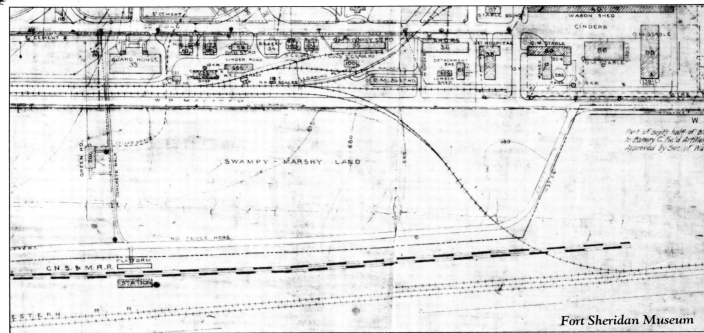

Fort Sheridan Museum

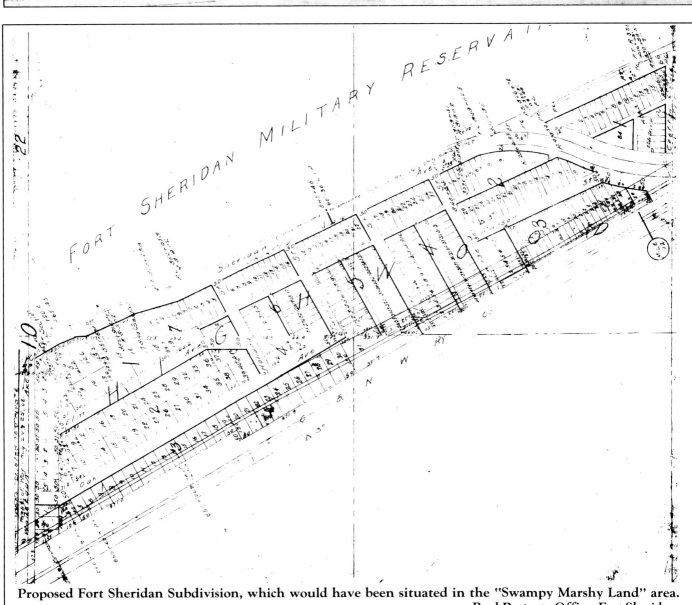

Proposed Fort Sheridan Subdivision, which would have been situated in the "Swampy Marshy Land" area.
Real Property Office, Fort Sheridan.

THE SIOUX INDIANS

After the Battle of Wounded Knee (South Dakota) on December 29, 1890, a band of Sioux Indians was escorted to Fort Sheridan by General Nelson A. Miles, the Commander of the Division of the Missouri. General Miles wished to impress the recently defeated tribes with the might of American civilization, so special entertainment was organized for them by the Evanston YMCA and the Illinois National Guard in Chicago. Unexpectedly, the Indians caught the fever of show business and all but four of the original band joined Buffalo Bill Cody's Wild West Show and toured Europe. Those remaining were sent back to the Pine Ridge, South Dakota, Indian reservation by the summer of 1891.[40]

Contrary to persistent rumors, Sitting Bull, the famous chief of the prairie Sioux, was not among the group. After the battle of the Little Big Horn, Sitting Bull and many of his followers went north into the British Northwest Territory, Dominion of Canada, and were at Fort Walsh in the Fall of 1876. The British government gave them refuge but no supplies and forbade them to make raids across the United States border.

The land around Fort Walsh was barren and game scarce. During the four years Sitting Bull and his followers lived there, they became impoverished and many died of starvation. By this time Sitting Bull had lost favor with the Sioux. He finally decided to surrender and was subsequently permitted to return to his place of birth, Grand River, South Dakota.

About 1889 rumors of a coming Indian Messiah caused unrest among the Sioux. The Indian agency believed that Sitting Bull would take advantage of the situation to regain his former position in the Sioux nation. Government agents considered this revelation a threat and attempted to have Sitting Bull arrested. On December 15, 1890, he was shot by Indian police while Sioux warriors tried to rescue him.[41]

HEADQUARTERS DIVISION OF THE MISSOURI

CHICAGO, ILLINOIS   March 13, 1891.

Colonel R. E. A. Crofton,

Fort Sheridan, Illinois.

Sir:

Colonel Cody has authority from Washington to take a number of Sioux, and as it is an opportunity that few Indians will have, I have no objection to his taking any of those at Fort Sheridan, provided they want to go. I believe it will be good employment for them and will educate them as to the extent, power, and numbers of the white race.

Please give him every facility for seeing and talking to them and let the Indians understand that it is at their own option, and if they go they do so voluntarily.

Very respectfully yours,

Major General, U. S. A.

Colonel R. E. A. Crofton assumed command of Fort Sheridan January, 1891. The letter is signed by Major General Nelson A. Miles. *Fort Sheridan Museum.*

1, White Beaver; 2, Plenty Wound; 3, Run By; 5, Short Bull; 6, Come and Grunt; 7, High Eagle; 8, Horn Eagle; 9, Sorrell Horse; 11, Standing Bear; 12, Lone Bull; 14, Close to Lodge; 15, One Star; 16, Know His Voice; 17, White Horse; 18, Take the Shield Away.

Fort Sheridan Museum.

THE CALL TO BOOTS AND SADDLE

In 1894 the soldiers at Fort Sheridan were again called upon to fulfill the post's protective role for Chicago and its citizens. The occasion was the Pullman Palace Car Company strike.

The Pullman Palace Car Company had built a village on Chicago's South side, a place where the company had a kind of birth to death grip on its employees. Union organizers were appalled at the "company town" atmosphere in Pullman Village and wanted to organize the workers. The company was somewhat less than receptive to the union overtures and disagreements ensued, disagreements which became violent when non-union employees went on strike in June, 1894. The soldiers at Fort Sheridan were ordered by President Grover Cleveland to re-establish order and prevent interference of the delivery of the mail. The presence of the Regulars was enough to deter further incidents.

Fort Sheridan assumed a different role when the battleship Maine was blown up and sank in Havana Harbor, February 15, 1898. The post became a troop movement center, funneling soldiers to the punitive Spanish American expedition. The infantry regiment assigned to Fort Sheridan never saw action. It was striken with an epidemic of fever while still in the port of embarkation at Tampa, Florida. The war lasted 109 days and cost the United States 2926 lives. Of these casualties, 361 died in battle or from wounds; the others died of disease.

After the Spanish American War, Fort Sheridan settled down and looked after itself and its building program. The Cavalry

LAKE FRONT PARK
JULY 7TH 1894.

was an integral part of the post, and Fort Sheridan became known in the local area as a "Cavalry" post.

The Cavalry were the aristocracy of soldiering. These were the gallant men in blue immortalized in dime store novels and nickelodeons, the hard-riding soldiers who always arrived in the nick of time. The Cavalry officer was glamorous and, for the times, relatively affluent. These credentials separately and in combination made the young Cavalry officer fair game for debutantes and other young women who aspired to be a dashing officer's lady.

Consequently, Fort Sheridan became one of the social centers of the North Shore during the pre-World War I period. A local travel folder from the period helps set the scene:

"The life at Fort Sheridan is that of any modern military post in time of peace. There are balls and receptions at the Officers' Club, small social affairs in the homes, the ceremony of guard mounting, drill and parade, band concerts, tennis, horseback riding, and a multitude of visitors from the civilian world to occupy the small amount of leisure time left to the officers from the round of routine work."

The account refers to the officer's life and its attendant prestige. The life of the average soldier was far less glamorous. Discipline was roughly handled and arbitrarily administered. The non-commissioned officers generally had a rudimentary education and held their positions more often by brawn and cunning than by brain and charm. At this point in the Army's history, less attention was paid to training and more to appearance.

The civil disorder in Mexico between 1910 and 1916 adversely affected American lives and interests. The possibility of war with Mexico and the war then beginning in Europe made Congress aware of our state of unpreparedness. The Army needed a drastic overhaul, and the War Department made sure that training and readiness became the watchwords of the day. This attitude was profoundly felt at Fort Sheridan and became a turning point in the post's history.

CHICAGO DAILY NEWS headline.

Troop tents at Lake Front Park, Chicago, during Pullman Palace Car Company strike. *Fort Sheridan Museum.*

THE PLATTSBURG PLAN

As part of the growing concern that a more viable military force was needed, the nation realized that a small standing army was simply not equal to the task of protecting the nation and its burgeoning population in a shrinking world. The concept of the citizen soldier had to be reestablished as an integral part of the total Army force — a stand-by force of men trained and prepared for deployment in case of war. Major General Leonard Wood, Commander, Department of the East between 1910 and 1914, believed future wars would see the greater part of the fighting done by these citizen soldiers. The soldiers to man this force would be young men who had just finished their schooling, prepared for their "fight in life" in civilian careers. General Wood's idea included a students' summer training camp independent of the state and National Guard structure.

In 1913 he caused two camps to be established as the training base for young men between the ages of 19 and 26. The first camp, a training center for the East Coast, was established at Gettysburg, Pennsylvania. General Wood felt this was especially appropriate since Gettysburg had been the site of the last great battle of the War Between the States, a battle fought by citizen soldiers much like the ones who would be trained. The second

camp was established at Monterey, California, and accommodated the young men who called the western states home. By 1915, the idea of the training camps was so popular that men over 26 clamored for the opportunity to attend a training camp and serve their country. General Wood set up the first camp for older men at Plattsburg, New York. The response was overwhelming. Business leaders and prominent civic and industrial leaders eagerly enrolled for their training. With their backing, the "Plattsburg Plan" received national attention and more applications. Requests poured in from all over the country asking for assistance in establishing similar camps. The first camp to use the highly successful "Plattsburg Plan" model was established at Fort Sheridan.[42]

Fort Sheridan held its first Reserve Officers' Training camp from May 15 to August 15, 1917. The second camp was held from August 27 to November 27, 1917. Enlistment was voluntary, and the ranks included congressmen, bankers, clergymen, mechanics, actors, farmers, athletes and musicians. During their short respites, some of the less experienced would employ a seasoned sergeant as a tutor of military tactics. He might have been a veteran of the War Between the States or a

Fort Sheridan Museum

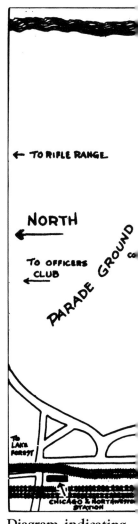

Diagram indicating location of trenches.

campaigner of one or more of the Indian wars. That experience was invaluable and earned for the non-commissioned officer a reputation of being the consummate soldier to his troops.

Just before the first session began training, Congress passed the National Defense Act of 1916, improving the camps by providing greater recognition from the government, payment of expenses to the men attending the camps, and establishing an Officers' Reserve Corps. Part of this improvement was due to the continuing public interest in what the camps were doing for the men. A greater portion of the camps' recognition came from the war then raging throughout Europe. There was belief in government circles the United States might be drawn into the conflict, and the government wanted to be sure the country was ready. That desire influenced the curricula the trainees studied.

There was trench warfare to master, and Fort Sheridan constructed and used an extensive trenching system simulating as closely as possible the trenches being employed in Europe.

Additionally, there was the science of communications: semaphore and wig-wag. There was also drill and horse care to master. The most common attitude was summed up by one participant that the trainees would make "no bone-headed

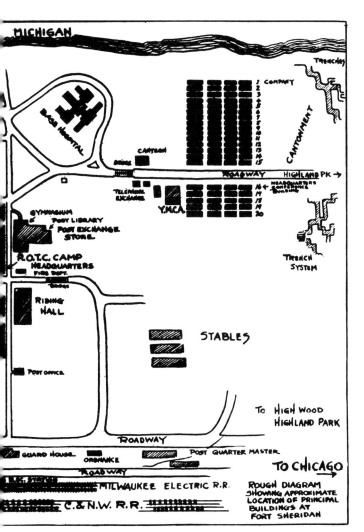

Fort Sheridan Museum.

move that might prevent a chance for a commission" in the Officers' Reserve Corps.

Colonel James A. Ryan, the commander of the second training camp, created two related actions to insure the men had the best possible chance of surviving the European battlefields. The first was a series of speakers who related to the trainees their experiences in the war zone. Some of the lecturers were from the staff of the school; others were visitors who gave "gripping" recitals of their war experiences, according to the newspaper accounts. Colonel Ryan also felt the soldiers he trained needed still more knowledge. In 1917 he commissioned a book, "Responsibility of the Officer for His Men." It would seem "The Commandant," as Colonel Ryan was usually called, was not only interested in the successful prosecution of war, but also the ethical prosecution of war and leadership of soldiers.

"This power of a nation is its trained manhood; without it we have to petition for peace, with it we dictate peace."[43]
    Brigadier General James A. Ryan
    1920

When the counting was done, approximately 5,800 men who completed three months' basic training in the two successive camps were commissioned as officers in the Army Reserve, applying in combat what they had learned from their training at Fort Sheridan. The camps provided a logical expansion into training centers following the Declaration of War on April 6, 1917. Fort Sheridan became an induction and midwest training center for men entering the Army from Illinois, Michigan and Wisconsin. The lessons learned in teaching the officers was applied to teaching the soldiers they would lead.

Fort Sheridan offered more than training to its "campers." It offered the hardy camaraderie of men forced to come to terms with themselves and the defense of their country. This fraternal spirit led to the formation of the Fort Sheridan Association. With the help and support of civilian businessmen, the Association was able to provide low-cost loans and stretched the new officer's dollar by engaging in volume buying of uniforms and other needed equipment. The Fort Sheridan Association formed a Home Service Department which gave assistance to the families of the men sent overseas and later formed the Bureau of Soldiers, Sailors and Marines to assist them to return to civilian life after the war. Just as importantly, the Association was a gratifying link to a waiting community that also supported "the boys over there." The concept of the Fort Sheridan Association was the first of its kind in the United States.[44]

There was a flurry of excitement on the post during the war. A Chicago Tribune article headlined: "Riding Teacher Seized as Spy at Fort's Gate." Edward W. Otto, believed to be a Hun officer and, in the secret service parlance, a "fixed post," opened an exclusive riding academy in Highland Park in 1918. His skill as an equestrian won him instant favor, and many of the children in the area became his pupils. Some of the parents, however, became suspicious when they observed that his route never varied and pupils reported that he took keen cognizance of everything transpiring at the post. Federal agents were informed and Otto was taken into custody on a charge of being a dangerous enemy alien after his riding academy was searched and incriminating evidence found.[45]

THE WORLD WARS:
CONFLICT AND PEACE

The "War to End All Wars" spread to engulf the civilized world. Local communities throughout the nation responded enthusiastically to the call to service. Servicemen's clubs were established, and soldiers were invited into private homes to share the hospitality of the local residents. One of the questions invariably asked was whether or not the soldier wanted a bath, a little known luxury of Army training.

Conservation was the order of the day: "Eat less, waste less" was a popular slogan. Hotels saved peach pits, olive stones and nut shells for making carbon for gas mask filters.[46] Dead leaves were saved and used to supplement the bedding of horses. A shortage of steel prevented the completion of the Michigan Avenue bridge in Chicago. The War Department was finally convinced the bridge was a "military necessity" because it was the most direct route between the city and Fort Sheridan. Steel was allocated; and bridge construction, which began in 1918, was completed with the bridge's dedication in 1920.[47]

On Fort Sheridan, mustering and training young men continued well into 1918. While the post continued its training role there were significant shifts in the wind. Wars produce casualties, and World War I was devastating. New and deadly innovations were introduced — war planes which occasionally preyed on the hapless foot soldier, and mustard gas which burned the skin and annihilated the lungs. Not all such casualties resulted in immediate death; and for those fortunate enough to survive, convalescence was needed. Fort Sheridan shifted its role to

accommodate these returning veterans. 1918 saw the construction and dedication of Lovell General Hospital and the assumption of post command by the Army Medical Department.

Lovell General Hospital, formerly General Hospital #28, was the largest base hospital established in the United States to treat wounded and convalescent soldiers. The wooden structures forming the hospital occupied most of the parade field as well as the entire tower complex of buildings. Between 1918 and the closing of the hospital in 1920, approximately 60,000 patients were treated. Most were released and returned to their homes. A few found their final home in the post cemetery.

A memento to the hospital's tenure is a sundial on the east lawn of the Commandant's private quarters. It was made by patients and presented to the post June 1, 1920.

Photographed by Nancy Powell, Fort Sheridan.

Lovell General Hospital.   *Training and Audio Visual Support Center (TASC), Fort Sheridan.*

The commander of Lovell General Hospital for its entire duration was Major Theodore S. Proxmire, father of United States Senator William Proxmire (Democrat, Wisconsin).[49] Lovell General Hospital was operative during the great influenza epidemic of 1918. While thousands of civilians were dying from the influenza, the fatalities at Fort Sheridan were few due to Major Proxmire's efforts. He was instrumental in obtaining and distributing an influenza preventive vaccine to volunteers in his hospital. His efforts and the dramatic results they gave are largely unrecorded by a populace that now takes flu vaccine for granted. Major Proxmire was from Lake Forest; and, according to Senator Proxmire, was the only doctor between Highland Park and Waukegan for a considerable period of time because of the service's demand for this specialized field.[50]

Even with Lovell General Hospital and other facilities, the intensity of World War I produced more casualties than the system could accommodate. Simply stated, there were not enough hospitals in the country to care for the sick and wounded. To alleviate this problem on a timely basis, the Acting Secretary of War, Hugh L. Scott, authorized procurement of hospital accommodations by leasing or purchasing existing buildings and authorized monies to make necessary alterations. Negotiations were made in the Chicago area for a lease contract and modifications of the nearly completed Field Museum. The contract provided a monthly rental of $5,208.33 and provided for a payment of $1,071,510.00 for necessary alterations to the facility. However, the war in Europe ground to a halt, the project was abandoned and the Field Museum restored to a pristine condition.[51]

In 1920 Lovell General Hospital was dismantled and sold under sealed bids. Fort Sheridan once again became a garrison for Infantry, Cavalry and Artillery units. The pastoral and peaceful life described in the pre-World War I era reasserted itself and enfolded the installation. From 1925 to 1939, Fort Sheridan was the site of the annual Fort Sheridan Horse Show. It was usually held on Labor Day at Gordon Johnston Field (now the east end of Gordon Johnston Drive).

In 1919 Hostess House of the Young Women's Christian Association was constructed from salvaged material. It provided recreation, a library and tea room for the soldiers and was operated by various women's groups who volunteered each day to serve tea and homemade food. While the reaction to the tea is not recorded, the soldiers were grateful for Hostess House and its domestic contribution to their well being. It occupied the west area of the parade ground for 24 years and was replaced by a Service Club, Building 205.

Major General William H. Carter. One of the oldest provisions of Army life is that a soldier who has made a career of the Army never really retires because he is subject to being recalled if the need arises. General Carter was recalled to active service in 1917 from "a nice quiet life up in the Blue Ridge Mountains of Virginia ... "I'm the only Civil War veteran called for service in this war."[48] General Carter commanded the Central Department headquartered in Chicago's Federal Building. He was sixty-six years old.

Hostess House.   *TASC, Fort Sheridan.*

General John J. Pershing, Commander-in-Chief of American forces in Europe during World War I, visiting Hostess House.   *Mrs. Barrett K. Mason, Highland Park.*

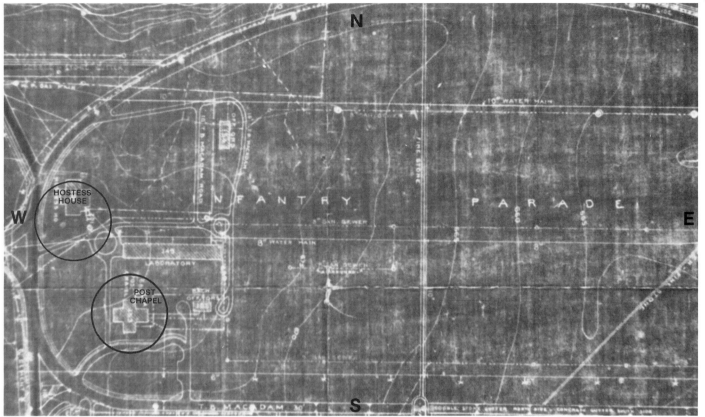

Fort Sheridan Museum.

Aerial view of the Horse Show Ring.

TASC, Fort Sheridan.

Exhibitions at horse show ring: The Cavalry performing a "monkey drill" and trick acrobatic riding.

TASC, Fort Sheridan.

The field artillerymen holding a driving contest with horse-drawn artillery and demonstrating a firing exhibition.

TASC, Fort Sheridan.

These teams not only performed exhibitions on the post but also at Soldiers' Field, Chicago Stadium, and at the World's Fair in 1933.

It was the last gasp of a heroic era. World War I saw the introduction of automobiles, tanks and trucks in battle. Army planners and thinkers already realized the days of the horse-drawn artillery and cavalry were limited. Mechanization was on its way. The field where the cavalry and artillery displayed their expertise with horses was converted to a ball park, and on June 9, 1944, the Fort Sheridan team had a successful game with the Chicago White Sox and defeated them, 8 to 6.[52]

Aside from the military units inhabiting the post, other units came and went. An example was the Bakers & Cooks School, which was established in 1921 and operated through World War II. Older local residents still remember the smell of freshly baked bread and of buying baked goods produced by the fledgling students. A school for automobile mechanics was also set up by the Quartermaster Corps in 1941. This school marked the end of an era as blacksmiths, wheelwrights and wagon-masters gave way to the all-purpose mechanic.

These schools were part of yet another shift in Fort Sheridan's emphasis. Training, which had begun in 1917 through the Reserve Officer Training Corps, became the post's primary mission. The effort gained further momentum through the Civilian Military Training Camps, an additional element of the 1920's and 1930's military preparedness.

The CMTC were incorporated into the National Defense Act of 1920 as a plan for domestic security. They were run by the Army on a strictly military basis for male inductees aged 17 to 24. The camps consisted of four weeks of intense training and had the ultimate goal of preparing the young men for commissioned or non-commissioned rank in the Army Reserve Corps or National Guard.

Fort Sheridan conducted its first CMTC in 1926, which was really a glorified tent city located on the site of what is now the Bolles Loop officer housing area.

Camp Leonard Wood.

TASC, Fort Sheridan.

The camps were referred to as "Paradise in Youth," but were in fact very little more than intense basic training centers. The camp at Fort Sheridan was named for General Leonard Wood to perpetuate his memory and foresight in conceiving and creating the training camps in 1917. General Wood was further honored by an arch donated by the Chicago Historical Society and the Military Training Camps Association. The arch came down in 1967 to make way for the housing area. From their inception until their demise in 1959, CMTC trained some 482,195 men nationwide.

TASC, Fort Sheridan.

Fort Sheridan was active during the depression era as a Civilian Conservation Corps (CCC) camp. The CCC was a federally subsidized program designed to provide jobs, lodging, training and subsistence for young men. Since the program was supervised by the Army, the camps had a quasi-military appearance. Many graduates of the program found their way into the Army. The CCC was actively involved in building and maintaining state and federal parks throughout the country. Many state and federal parks owe their road networks, signposts, carefully constructed woodland habitats and other features to the work done by the young men of the Civilian Conservation Corps.

Regular Army training remained an element at Fort Sheridan during the period between 1920 and 1943. A primary part of the training was establishing a major training center for the Coast Artillery (anti-aircraft). The program was part of a sweeping reorganization of the entire War Department to foster a closer relationship between air and ground fighting. Occasionally eager young soldiers would fire their batteries at drones flown over Lake Michigan before checking to make sure their work was correct. Sometimes that created a public relations problem for the Army. Such was the case in October, 1922, when four high-velocity shells crashed through the roof and walls of the Francis C. Farwell estate, north of the installation. Fortunately, no one was home at the time.[53]

The soldiers of the anti-aircraft units lived in the tent village that was part of Camp Leonard Wood. Winter time insulation was somewhat scarce and snow often piled up inside the tents. Toothpaste tubes and shoe polish had to be thawed before being used. Water had to be melted before the men could shave, and most soldiers slept with their pressed and folded uniforms in the bunk so they could dress rapidly in time for Reveille. The camp was known as "Little Siberia," but the discomforts were no excuse for missing formations.

In 1941 the anti-aircraft companies expanded into an anti-aircraft brigade. The post utilized a twenty-five foot Chris Craft as a deterrant against any mishaps. Docked at Great Lakes, it was used to ward off other ships that might be in line of anti-aircraft fire and retrieved airplane targets.[54]

From 1936 forward, Fort Sheridan found itself enmeshed in the process of getting ready for World War II. Despite isolationist tendencies, evidence from the period clearly indicated there was large scale agreement in high government circles the United States would be drawn into the conflict. Preparations were quietly begun in several parts of the country to ease the transition from peace to conflict.

In 1940, as the war in Europe continued to intensify, the peacetime draft was initiated in the United States. Fort Sheridan became one of four Recruit Reception Centers in the country and was the first post to receive the "selectees." (The "dog tag" punching machine that was used to identify the selectees is still used by the post.) The Recruit Reception Center (Building 443) was referred to as "Boomtown," and Fort Sheridan prepared to receive the prospective soldiers as they poured into the area and were processed into the Army as the war escalated.

Dog-tag Punching Machine.

31

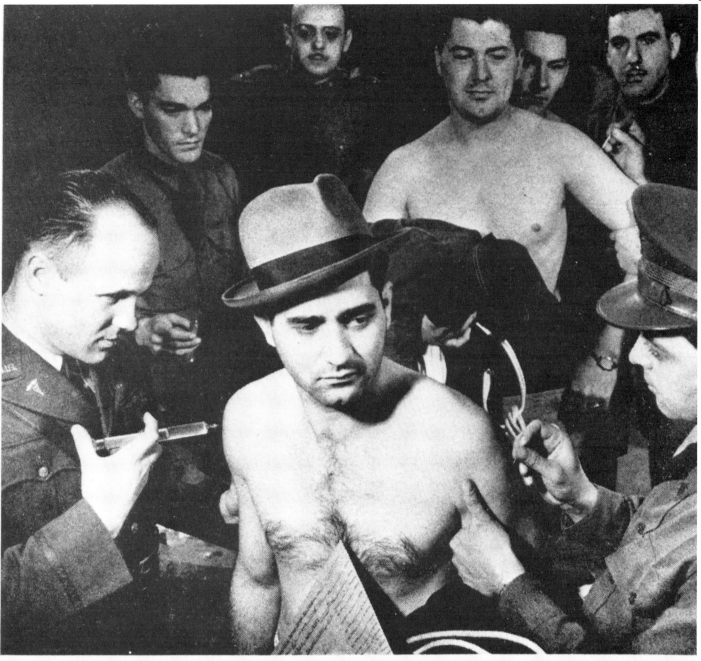

RELUCTANT PREPAREDNESS in the U.S. began with first peacetime draft in November 1940 and civilians learned all about mysteries of inductions and mass inoculations.

LIFE magazine, 25th Anniversary issue.

Fort Sheridan had the war-time distinction of receiving the second group of Women's Army Auxiliary Corps, or WAAC, soldiers. They arrived Christmas night, 1942, from the WAAC Training Center at Fort Des Moines, Iowa. Their arrival might have been a first, but they could not be sent here until after Christmas because of a shortage of winter clothing. (The first group sent from the training center went to Fort Sam Houston, Texas).[55] They were housed in a building located behind the Community Club, just north of the ravine in the vicinity of what is now the third fairway. There was much ado in preparing for their arrival. They were provided with mahogany dining room furniture and latrines painted butter yellow. Bedsheets were quickly pressed into service and draperies hung to accommodate the ladies' amenities and preserve their dignity. Fort Sheridan also welcomed the arrival of one of the first black WAC (Women's Army Corps) detachments, November, 1943. They were under the command of First Lieutenant Mildred B. Osby and performed clerical duties at the Recruit Reception Center. (The designation, WAC, was adopted in 1943.)

Special mention must be made of the many kindnesses lavished upon Fort Sheridan's soldiers by civilian neighbors during World War II. A group of generous men from Glencoe, Illinois, organized the Fort Sheridan Volunteer Committee. Money to finance this committee was raised by subscription to coordinate and finance civilian activities on post.

Another group of concerned civilians formed the Fort Sheridan Tower, Incorporated, to sponsor the post newspaper. This non-profit organization used the proceeds from advertising to contribute to the post's educational and recreational fund. Neighbors' generosity extended to furnishing dayrooms, contributing books to the library, and furnishing entertainment. Even that well-traveled trouper, Bob Hope and his show, appeared at the post to entertain the troops, September, 1944.[56]

This was another time for being conservative, and the theme was "Waste Not Want Not." One of the Army's conservation ideas was to turn in clothes at the first sign of wear so they could be

In FORMATION, a group of Waacs enter their barracks at Fort Sheridan. The company, loaded down with baggage, arrived from Fort Des Moines, Iowa, yesterday to serve as stenographers, clerks and typists. They will do their own cooking and kitchen police.

repaired before being worn out. There was an array of garbage cans outside Fort Sheridan's mess halls, but they were not for waste: One was for tin cans (11,400 pounds were collected for re-cycling); another was for grease and tallow which was rendered into glycerin for the manufacture of gun powder; uneaten soft food was collected by contractors who raised hogs; animal bones were ground up for fertilizer.[57] Twenty-five pounds of pure zinc and copper were turned in as salvage by the Post Public Relations Office. The metal came from engravings used in TOWER newspaper pictures. The wood blocks on which the cuts were mounted were burned, leaving the highly critical war materials.[58]

The Recruit Reception Center and Anti-Aircraft Artillery training received the greater part of attention and publicity during the first two years of World War II. Then as now, the performance of soldiers in combat influenced how they were trained. In this war, it turned out that physical requirements needed to become more strenuous. Part of that training involved setting up and utilizing an infiltration course. The course was established in 1943 and took soldiers through a simulated battlefield, climbing over shell holes, under barbed wire and around other obstacles with machine gun fire whistling overhead and dynamite charges booming in their ears. The training was realistic and prepared young soldiers for the test they would face. The infiltration course became a standard training device during World War II and has continued to be an integral part of the soldier's training to the present day.

Fort Sheridan continued training anti-aircraft artillery units through 1943 when the post changed from an Army Ground Forces installation to an Army Service Forces installation taking in responsibility for Illinois, Michigan and Wisconsin. What that meant for the post was that it no longer trained troops for combat but supplied personnel and equipment to support the combat forces.

Chicago Sun Staff Photo
TASC, Fort Sheridan.

34

By the time the anti-aircraft training center completed its span of life, twenty battalions, two groups and one regiment of anti-aircraft artillery had been trained at Fort Sheridan.

The Army Service Forces were particularly interested in rehabilitating and reconditioning soldiers who were having difficulty in their adjustment to Army life. Disciplinary offenders were sent to a Rehabilitation Center established at the south end of the post, retrained and ultimately returned to active duty. This was not the only facility designed to help the soldier. A Training Center was established to provide basic education — the 3 R's — for those who needed it. An Orientation Center was also established to provide further educational benefits.

The Recruit Reception Center suspended activities May 29, 1943, but was reactivated on November 6, 1943, as part of the National Selective Service Act. Fort Sheridan became a recruiting nucleus for Illinois, Michigan and Wisconsin during the balance of the war. The WAC personnel continued to contribute their talents, and it is believed the first WAC's to reenlist in the Army did so at Fort Sheridan: PFC Shirley Slaughter and CPL Harriett B. Lutwak, both of whom were from Chicago.[59]

In 1944 Fort Sheridan assumed administrative control for prisoner of war camps in Illinois, Michigan and Wisconsin. A total of 15,000 prisoners under this administrative control performed civilian construction jobs, crop harvesting, kitchen

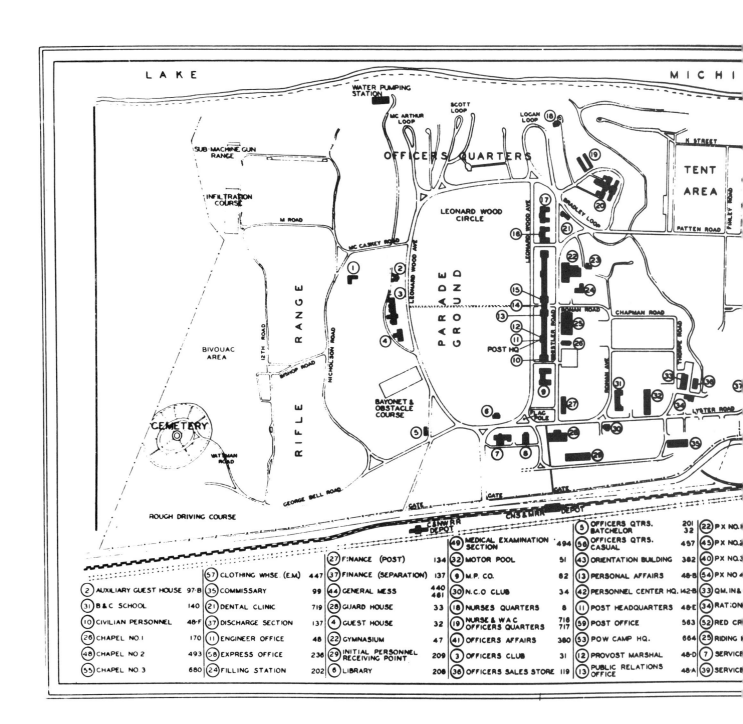

police and other forms of manual labor.

On the Fort Sheridan installation itself the prisoners were housed in the area vacated by the Rehabilitation Center.

They were paid eighty cents a day in canteen coupons as specified in the Geneva Convention. At the Chemical Warfare Warehouse in Chicago, some of the POW dissassembled canisters and carriers from used gas masks. Their work was considered urgent because of the pressing need to salvage every possible bit of crude rubber. This salvage program would have been unlikely if POW labor had not been available.[60] After World War II all but nine POW from Fort Sheridan were

repatriated to their homeland; those nine are buried in the post cemetery.

Information about the Prisoner of War camps is sketchy. They existed and the prisoners were all incarcerated after Operation Overlord began capturing large numbers of Axis soldiers. According to an account by a former POW, Axis soldiers preferred to surrender to advancing American soldiers because of their humane treatment. This former POW arrived in the United States on the Queen Mary and was interned at Camp Grant, Rockford, Illinois. His story seems to reflect a common experience among Axis POW: He was surprised to be issued new clothing that fit well and that he didn't have to launder himself; new bedding for beds with mattresses and springs, as opposed to the straw sacks he was accustomed to. He also related that he received his first pair of reading glasses at Camp Grant and was able to attend educational classes.

By the end of 1945 the prisoners of war in the United States had performed work valued at $8,894,795.00, and of the 360,000 22 escaped, 20 of whom were recaptured.[61]

As World War II drew to a close, the Army became concerned about out-processing the soldiers it had in-processed. At Fort Sheridan that meant closing the Recruit Reception Center and making it a Separation Center. The transformation took place within a week. In 1944 the Separation Center was one of the first and busiest in the country with daily troop trains arriving alongside Building 209, the Initial Receiving Point station. Incoming personnel would acquire their records, receive orientation, fill out locator cards and get bunk assignments. Among the first to arrive was a group of liberated American POW who arrived in April, 1945, directly from overseas.[62]

Between the Recruit Reception Center and the Separation Center, Fort Sheridan processed approximately half a million men and women into and out of the Army including the first soldier separated through the point system of demobilization.[63] (The point system was designed to individualize discharges, giving credit for time served, combat decorations, and parenthood).

Fort Sheridan Museum.

THE HEADQUARTERS

During World War II Fort Sheridan was part of the Sixth Service Command. In 1946 the Service Commands were abolished and replaced with six continental Army areas. Chicago was headquarters for the Fifth United States Army and remained so until 1967 when the headquarters moved to Fort Sheridan. Geographically, Fifth Army was the largest of the Continental United States Armies encompassing thirteen states. It was activated at Oujda, Morocco, January 5, 1943, under the command of Lieutenant General Mark W. Clark. Fifth Army subsequently transferred its headquarters to its present home at Fort Sam Houston, Texas, in 1971.

Fort Sheridan was a primary reception center during the Korean conflict of the 1950's and an administrative and logistics center during the Vietnam conflict.

More recently, the post was headquarters to the Military Enlistment Processing Command (MEPCOM), which is responsible for operating the Military Enlistment Processing Stations (MEPS) throughout the country. MEPCOM completed its move to Great Lakes Naval Training Center in January, 1983.

Fort Sheridan is headquarters for the United States Army Recruiting Command (USAREC) which is responsible for providing the enlisted personnel strength of the Active Army and the United States Army Reserve, including nurses and candidates for Warrant Officer Flight Training and Officer Candidate School. USAREC Headquarters was relocated to Fort Sheridan in 1973 from Hampton, Virginia.

Also located at Fort Sheridan is the United States Army Fourth Recruiting Brigade (MIDWEST), which is responsible for recruiting activities in all or parts of eleven states in the north central United States. One of the Fourth Recruiting Brigade's

Lieutenant General Edward C. Peter receives the Fourth United States Army flag from General Robert W. Sennewald, Commander of the United States Army Forces Command. Command Sergeant Major Charles W. Atkins waits to recover the flag. October 1, 1984.

subordinate commands, the United States Army Recruiting Battalion Chicago, is also based at Fort Sheridan. The battalion is responsible for recruiting activities in Lake, Cook and DuPage counties in Illinois.

In 1973, Fort Sheridan became headquarters for Army Readiness and Mobilization Region V (ARMR V), which was one of nine such commands in the continental United States. Its mission was to improve the readiness of United States Army Reserve and National Guard forces in the Region's five state area of Illinois, Iowa, Minnesota, Wisconsin and Missouri.

On October 1, 1984, ARMR V was deactivated and Fort Sheridan became headquarters for the newly-activated Fourth United States Army. Fourth Army was activated in August, 1932, at Omaha, Nebraska, and was part of four Continental United States Army structures established by the War Department. On June 18, 1936, the headquarters was moved to the Presidio of San Francisco, California.

In 1941, the War Department assigned Fourth Army the mission of establishing the Western Defense Command for the defense of the Pacific Coast, to include Alaska, and was subsequently designated as the Western Defense Command and Fourth Army. After the attack on Pearl Harbor in December, 1941, the Fourth Air Force was added to the command along with additional ground forces.

On September 18, 1943, Fourth Army was separated from the Western Command and reorganized at San Jose, California. Eventually the headquarters moved to Fort Sam Houston, Texas, where it remained until it was deactivated in June, 1971. On October 1, 1984, Fourth Army was reactivated and headquartered at Fort Sheridan.

Throughout its existence, the mission of Fourth Army has been training and continental defense. Over half of the combat soldiers deployed overseas in World War II were trained by Fourth Army. Fourth Army also responded to the Cuban missile crisis in October, 1962, by deploying units to the Florida coast — one of the largest peacetime emergency troop moves in United States history.

Today, Fourth Army supervises the training and readiness of some 128,000 reserve component soldiers as well as exercising continental defense responsibilities for seven midwestern states: Illinois, Indiana, Iowa, Michigan, Ohio, Wisconsin and Minnesota).

The United States Army Garrison at Fort Sheridan provides administrative and logistical support for all assigned personnel, post activities and tenant units. The garrison also provides administrative, logistical and maintenance requirements for physical facilities and equipment at Army Reserve centers throughout Indiana, Illinois, Michigan and a portion of southeast Wisconsin.

While its functional form and reason for being are unique from a historical point of view, Fort Sheridan still continues to play a leading role in the United States Army.

ESSENTIAL FOR FREEDOM SINCE 1887.

Public Affairs Office, Fourth Army.

Work to create the Fourth Army red and white insignia began in 1926 when a unit insignia for the Continental United States Army was suggested. No specific records appear to exist explaining the use of the square set on end with four-leaf clover inset as the basic design. The United States Army Institute of Heraldry presumes that the scheme was adopted to carry out an obvious tie to the number "four."

Part Two

THE HISTORIC DISTRICT AND ITS ARCHITECTS

One of the final acts of violence in subduing the American Indian occurred at the Battle of Wounded Knee. By that time the buffalo herds were practically extinct and the plains were being homesteaded by settlers. These events were preceded by a national policy of closing temporary frontier posts and establishing permanent military garrisons at strategic points throughout the United States.

Fort Sheridan is the first regimental-scale post established east of the Mississippi River that was planned and constructed during this period of transition and one of the first Army posts built without a surrounding defensive barricade.[64] Formerly, frontier forts had encircling wooden or earthen perimeters. These perimeters were built to protect soldiers from hostile attack and to provide a base from which they could conduct an attack. In a sense, the frontier outposts were like European castles adapted for different climates, different times and different needs. Fort Sheridan did not require this design; its initial mission was to defend the citizens of Chicago, twenty-five miles south of the installation.

It was not until 1965 that an effort was made by former Fort Sheridan Museum curator, Marie L. D'Elia (United States Army Master Sergeant, retired), to declare Fort Sheridan a National Historic Landmark and therefore nationally significant in the history of the United States. Shortly after a formal inquiry was made to the National Park Service, Department of Interior, the entire legal and bureaucratic structure governing historic preservation was altered and Fort Sheridan's official historical recognition was postponed. Instead, the National Trust for Historic Preservation established a National Register of Historic Places. Under this preservation program of the National Park Service, the Fort Sheridan Tower was separately placed on the Register, December 4, 1974.

In 1977, the concept of an historic district was introduced to not only recognize Fort Sheridan's historical resources but all of its architecturally significant buildings as well.[65] Early in 1979 the post underwent an Historic American Buildings Survey. As a result of this survey, ninety-four buildings, to include the Water Tower, were designated as one National Historic District and placed as such upon the National Register of Historic Places, September 29, 1980.

It was not until October 29, 1984, that Fort Sheridan was finally immortalized by being recognized as a National Historic Landmark. The historic district as defined follows very closely the original plan of the installation and consists of approximately 230 acres.

Fort Sheridan is one of the few posts in the United States Army designed by notable architectural and landscaping firms. The firm of Holabird and Roche (now Holabird and Root, Chicago) dates from 1883 and is known primarily for its pioneer work in the use of the skeleton frame and in the construction of the early skyscrapers. Architect William Holabird was the son of Quartermaster General of the Army, Samuel Holabird. William attended West Point from 1873 to 1875 and resigned for personal reasons. He then came to Chicago to study his chosen profession and eventually formed a partnership with Martin Roche.

To Captain Crosby Miller, Quartermaster Corps, was entrusted the execution of the work. The first thirty-seven buildings were contracted with Pease, Appleton and Williams, known as Williams and Company. This company failed financially, and there followed a succession of eight other private contractors.

The original specifications stated: "Except it be otherwise specified, all materials are to be of the best quality of their respective kinds, and all labor is to be done in the most thorough and workmanlike manner to the full satisfaction of the officer in charge. As the government desires only the best of material and workmanship, should poor brick, stone, black-knot lumber or any other low-grade stuff be used, the work will be condemned." It was also specified that all fireplaces be boarded up after working hours so that the workmen would not use them.

Part of the unity of the buildings and grounds comes from the landscape architect, Ossian C. Simonds, who was associated with Holabird and Roche until 1883. He was a practitioner of the prairie style of landscaping, using wide open spaces reminiscent of the prairies.[66] Unity is further enhanced by Fort Sheridan's plan, the so-called "hollow square" — buildings constructed around a common area, the parade field. The focal point is the landmark water tower, flanked by what were originally Cavalry, Infantry and Artillery barracks.

The separation of rank was traditional, with the troop areas at the south side of the square, officer housing at the east side, bachelor officer housing and the officers' open mess at the north side, and the west side comprising the entrance to the post. The hospital, stables and the majority of those other buildings necessary to support the operation of a military installation are removed from the common area.

The ribbon-like rows of recessed arched windows and wide arches around entrances that Holabird and Roche used suggest the prevalent influence of the architect H. H. Richardson, referred to as Richardsonian Romanesque. The brick work forming arches, friezes, cornices and brackets provide the majority of the decorative detail. The roofs were originally slate, and copper was used extensively in the downspouts and on the porch roofs. The buildings were constructed with indoor plumbing and coal-fired steam heat. Even though electricity was available and was most likely used in some of the buildings, records indicate mineral oil was a popular and economical source of early lighting.

All the buildings in the historic district were constructed between 1889 and 1910: sixty-six were designed by Holabird and Roche; twenty-six were designed from plans issued by the Quartermaster General of the Army; one was designed by a post engineer; and the architect of one of the buildings is unknown. The unusual buff cream color of the bricks, fired on site, comes from their age and high lime content.

Alterations have come about mostly on the interior as the buildings were adapted for functions for which they were not built.

Exterior alterations include replacement of brick, removing chimneys and cupolas, enlarging and squaring off arched doorways, partial or complete in-filling of windows and doors or adding additional windows and doors and enclosing porches.

Mr. Holabird's specifications did not allow for much bowing to the popular Victorian architectural styles of the day except for the two commandants' quarters, a classic adaptation of the Queen Anne style characterized by a domed turret, third floor projecting gables and columned porches.

Some of the temporary buildings constructed during World War II are scattered throughout the historic district and referred to accordingly, but the majority remain standing at the south end of the post outside the boundaries of the historic district. They were constructed from standardized plans and are easily recognized by their long, barrack-type design. They served as mess halls, barracks, and as administrative, recreational and medical facilities.[67] A map that best illustrates this era is on pages 35 and 36.

It is interesting to note that a permanent chapel was not included in Fort Sheridan's original plans. Apparently services were held in Buildings 60 and 47 prior to a chapel being built at the west end of the parade field and destroyed by fire in 1931. The present chapel on Patten Road became the only functioning chapel October 1, 1977, when worship service was consolidated for both Catholics and Protestants. This one, along with two other wood frame chapels, was constructed in 1941.

POST CHAPEL. FT SHERIDAN. ILL.

The location of the Post Chapel is identified on the map on page 28. *Fort Sheridan Museum.*

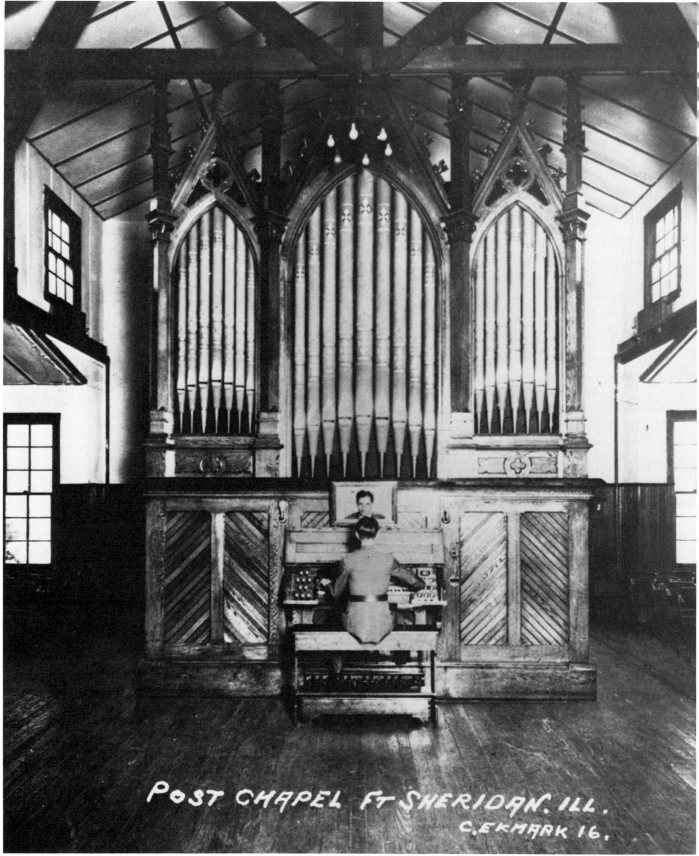

POST CHAPEL FT SHERIDAN, ILL.
C. EKMARK 16.

The chapel organ was destroyed in the 1931 fire.

Fort Sheridan Museum.

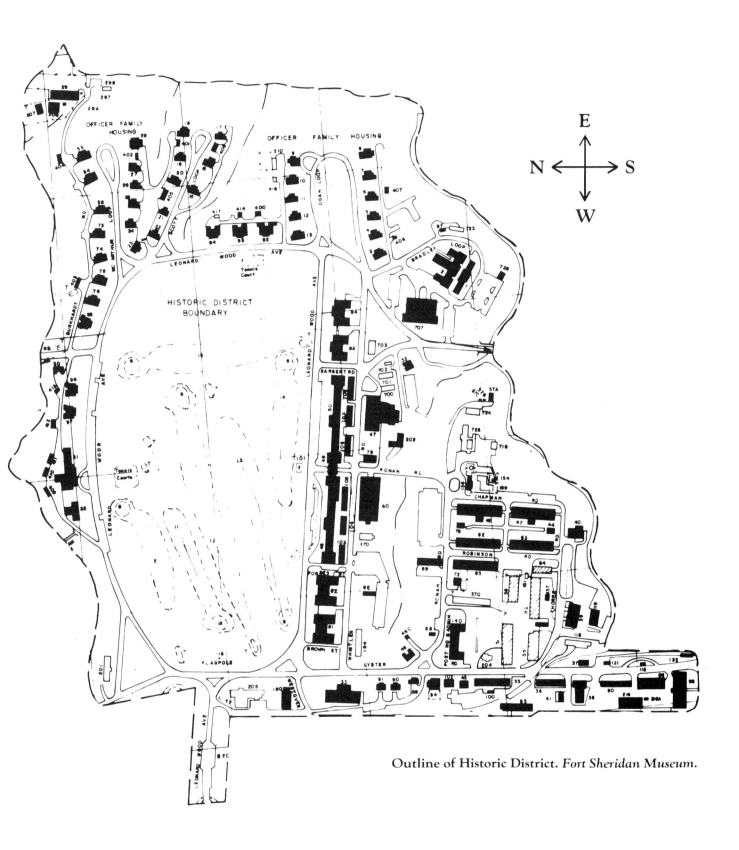

Outline of Historic District. *Fort Sheridan Museum.*

THE BUILDINGS, ANECDOTES AND GHOSTS

It is easiest to enter Fort Sheridan from Sheridan Road through George Bell Gate, an iron gate that still functions.

One of the first things a visitor sees is the flagpole directly in line with the main entrance. The flag epitomizes the pledge each soldier takes to support and defend our nation against all enemies, foreign and domestic.

While most soldiers tell time today by their own watch, it was not that way in the Army during the founding days of Fort Sheridan. A bugler announced the soldier's day which began with "Reveille," the time to be up and about; and, at the same time, the flag of the United States was raised. In reverse manner, the working day ended with "To The Colors" and "Retreat" when the flag was lowered.

On Army installations all over the world it is still tradition and regulation to render honors when the flag is raised and lowered. Between the beginning and the ending of the work day, the soldier will hear "Mess Call" in the morning, at noon and in the evening. He will also hear "Work Call" after breakfast and after the noon meal. Even when the day is over, the soldier still hears the sounds of the bugle: "Call to Quarters," "Lights Out," and at the official end of the day when "Taps" is played. Today's bugler at Fort Sheridan is usually electronic, but the function is still the same.

In January, 1972, the gate was closed to about t̶
They had marched from Lincoln Park, Chicago, and se̶
issues as the Vietnam war, substandard housing and aborti̶

Chicago Indian Village demonstration.

TASC, Fort Sheridan.

ns who called themselves the Chicago Indian Village.
campment at George Bell Gate to protest such social
TASC, Fort Sheridan.

Just beyond the main entrance is a small guardhouse for the Military Police personnel who perform the same functions as the police force in any metropolitan area. The guardhouse shelters the Military Police as they direct traffic and provide security for the post. Their function has remained the same through the years, but the guardhouse has been fairly mobile. During the earliest part of the fort's history, it was located on the north side of the main gate and was, in fact, a holding station. During the post's intervening years, the guardhouse has slowly migrated to the south side of the main gate, its present location, with an intermediate stop in the middle of the roadway.

Military Police holding station located on the north side of George Bell Gate.   *TASC, Fort Sheridan.*

In this section, several historic buildings will be discussed in some detail. In most cases there will be two photographs of a building in order to compare its originality with the alterations that have taken place over the years. Each building in the historic district will be identified on a map on page 42 by its number. The buildings in the housing areas have two numbers, the building number and the street address. They will be referred to by their building number and assumed designation. Identification numbers are an orderly way for the Army to keep an up-to-date inventory, not only of its buildings, but every soldier and every piece of equipment.

From that beginning and beyond the old Service Club (Building 205), The Tower can be seen — the building most people notice most often.

West of The Tower complex are Buildings **81** and **82.** These buildings and their duplicates (Buildings 83 and 84) on the east end of the long tower complex, form bookends for the tower complex itself and lend a graceful kind of symmetry to the layout of the installation. These four buildings were built in 1905 from standardized plans then used by the Quartermaster General of the Army and have served as Cavalry and Artillery barracks. They now serve as administrative buildings for some of the various units on the post.

Buildings **48** and **50**, flanking either side of the water tower, were designed by Holabird and Roche and built in 1890. They were also used as barracks. Each housed almost 500 Infantry soldiers and the soldiers necessary for administrative and supply support. Later, Building 48 (the western building of the two) was converted to artillery barracks and also accommodated the Coast Artillery band, Post Headquarters and a machine gun room in the basement. When Fifth United States Army resided at Fort Sheridan from 1967 to 1971, Building 48 became its headquarter as noted by the plaque:

"Headquarters, Fifth United States Army, Relocated from Chicago to Fort Sheridan, Illinois, May 19, 1967, Lt. General J.H. Michaelis, Commander."

Tower Complex: Buildings 48, 49 and 50, 1889-1890.

All traces of their original use as barracks have been removed, including the fireplaces and cupolas, and they now accommodate administrative offices.

The approximately fifty-four acres north of The Tower really are a parade field and not simply a cleverly disguised golf course. The parade field has been used for drill (considered a tactical battlefield exercise and not necessarily a ceremonial function), parades and military ceremonies since the founding of Fort Sheridan.

The layout here is very logical and very Army, harking back to the separation of ranks discussed earlier. Before the bugler sounded "Reveille," the soldiers would assemble on the parade field. Usually, companies were housed together so each company would form up in front of its portion of the barracks. At the appropriate time, the officers would appear from their quarters, everyone would be accounted for, the roll call would be reported, "Reveille" accomplished, and the orders for the day given.

Then the soldiers would return to their barracks for "police of the area," cleaning up by any other name, and the work day would proceed in its established fashion. At the end of the day, everyone would assemble again, "Retreat" would be sounded with all its pomp and pageantry, the soldiers would return to the field mess for dinner and the officers to the officers' mess, the Army's name for a dining hall.

While Army life is not that circumscribed today, that type routine and discipline have enriched Fort Sheridan with an assortment of anecdotes. Perhaps none is more locally known nor more honored than the story of the milk wagon horse.

TASC, Fort Sheridan.

During World War I, Building 81 was a rehabilitation and education center. Some of the classes included art, tailoring, penmanship, and poultry raising.

Reproduced from the original photograph by Nancy Powell, Fort Sheridan.

Commercial Artists at Work U.S.A. General Hospital No. 28, Fort Sheridan, Ill.

TASC, Fort Sheridan

In the days when the Army moved its services and supplies by horse, it was customary to sell the older animals when they were past their prime. One must remember the Cavalry was the epitome of the Army and very aware of its own image, an image it carried to the uniforms it wore, the horses it rode, and the swagger it adopted.

The story, perhaps apocryphal, goes that at one of these sales a former Cavalry mount was sold to a local Highwood, Illinois, milkman.

Whether for man or horse, the transition from Cavalry to milk route was traumatic. The sale was consummated and the transition made. One day, as luck would have it, horse, owner and milk wagon were passing Fort Sheridan when "Assembly" was sounded, the bugle calling men and animals to their formation before "Work Call" sounded. The horse heard the bugle call and reacted instinctively, racing toward the parade field dragging wagon and owner along.

The horse assumed its old place and stood at the best attention a proud Cavalry mount can when encumbered by an irate owner and a mostly destroyed milk wagon. According to the story, the Cavalry troop commander purchased the horse on the spot and reimbursed the milkman for his damages. The re-enlisted horse was duly reclassified and placed on limited, over-age status so it could step to the sounds of the bugle for the rest of its life.[69]

The Tower.   *Highland Park Historical Society.*

Before Building **49**, The Tower, was built between 1889 and 1890, tons of cement were poured into the foundation to withstand the structure's weight.[70] It was designed by Holabird and Roche to house the fort's water supply and to help control water pressure using a gravity feed water system.

The water tower remains the dominant structure on post and one of the North Shore's prominent landmarks. The tower was originally 227 feet 10 inches and is said to have been modeled after the Campanile (Bell Tower) in St. Mark's Square, Venice, Italy. In 1928 the first floor above the arch was modified to accommodate a telephone exchange. The switchboard was used regularly until 1944 and is now displayed at the Fort Sheridan Museum. In 1944 this area was again remodeled and sound-proofed for the post's short-lived radio station and band rehearsal room. In 1949 significant structural weaknesses forced the building to be remodeled, removing some 60 feet from the tower's height, modifying the roofline and replacing the wooden staircase with a circular steel staircase.

There are 225 steps from the base to the top, covering most of the tower's current 167 feet 5 inches height. The tower continues to perform its original function. Its 90,000 gallon water tank still functions as a water source for the post and is one of the water supplies used by the Fire House.

The tower's massive stone arched opening, the sally port, was designed to allow a platoon of forty-four soldiers to march through. The floral motif on the ceiling of the sally port is similar to the design on Buildings 8 and 9. It was also designed with recessed vestibules to protect passers-by from the carriages and wagons traveling on the main roadway that was routed through the post and connected Chicago with Milwaukee and Green Bay.

East from the tower stands the other half of the building bookends, Buildings **83** and **84**. Building 83, the counterpart of Building 81, was part of a project the War Department called a Regional Station Hospital. At the end of World War II, these Regional Station Hospitals were responsible for treating many specialized cases formerly transferred to a general hospital. Various civilian individuals and organizations cooperated in remodeling the building for an occupational therapy and remedial facility to help convalescent patients return to a normal life.

During World War II, Building 84 housed the WAC medical detachment and in 1971 became Headquarters for the United States Army Veterinary School. Remodelling has taken its toll and not much remains indicating Buildings' 83 and 84 original function. However, Building 84 still retains what appears to be the original oak staircase, camouflaged by several coats of paint.

On the south side of Leonard Wood Avenue, the street bounding the parade field, are the areas where the soldiers lived and performed the majority of their work. Recall for a moment that an Army post is a small city unto itself. It has its own police and fire force, its own department store (Main Exchange), its own grocery store (a Commissary), medical facilities — most things one would associate with a small, well structured city.

From Leonard Wood Avenue, the tour continues onto Bradley Loop and Buildings **1** and **2**, the old Fort Sheridan Hospital and once part of Lovell General Hospital and Regional Station Hospital. Building 1 was constructed in 1893 from standardized plans of the Surgeon General's Office. It was designed as a 2½ story central block with 2 single story side wings. At that time, a wide veranda covered the main facade and wings, used for the often prescribed fresh-air treatment.

Three wings were constructed on the north side between 1905 and 1911, raising the capacity from 62 to 102 beds. These wings were connected to the main hospital by a passageway. When the passageway was removed in 1952, the wings became Building 2.

Buildings 1 and 2: Hospital complex, wards and Isolation Hospital. *TASC, Fort Sheridan.*

Like many hospitals throughout the country, the Fort Sheridan hospital grew in fits and starts. A cell room was completed in 1925 in the central block of the basement in Building 1 and is still intact. In 1929 a single story brick entryway was added to the center of the building and iron bars were installed in the prison ward, located in the basement of the east wing; this area is now used for office space. A water cistern in the basement is believed to have been the post's original water supply; it is now sealed. The skylights that once illuminated the operating theater have been removed.

Buildings 1 and 2 were used for medical purposes until 1967 when the clinics were relocated to Building 707, just west. Building 1 was redesignated as the post's library while Building 2 retained some of its original medical uses and gathered additional functions. What used to be wards now house the Education Center (Ward D), Veterinary Services and classrooms (Ward C), and the Preventive Medicine Activity and classrooms (center wing which formerly accommodated the squad room of the hospital corps).

An isolation hospital was once part of the old hospital complex. Records indicate it was completed in 1912 and was still standing as late as 1943. The isolation hospital stood to the north of what was once Ward C; it is unknown when it was demolished.

Building 1, the old Fort Sheridan Hospital.

Highland Park Historical Society.

Building 1, the Post Library.

TASC, Fort Sheridan.

The library itself has been fairly mobile over the years. Prior to its present location and branch facilities, it was located in a section of the Hostess House. In 1943 it moved to Building 208, the only building on the parade field at that time. See map on page 35.

Within the boundaries of the historic district a few stories have circulated about its former employees. One in particular involves a custodian of the old hospital who apparently still feels a sense of responsibility. This particular ethereal spirit reportedly is dressed in dark clothing and carries a heavy object. However, if anyone happens to be working overtime in this building late at night, he can be assured that the custodian he may encounter is only tending to the worker's comfort by stoking the furnace and tapping the radiators.[71]

To the east of the old hospital stands the morgue, Building 87. It is easily identified by the blind windows, two of which flank the entrance with stone crosses in high relief. The morgue contained a sink, sewer, and water system for performing autopsies and was illuminated by a skylight. This one-room building is now used for storage. Here is an interesting divergence in Army economies. While Buildings 1 and 2 were built from standardized plans, Building 87 was designed by the architectural firm of Holabird and Roche and was also built in 1893.

Building 87.

Building 87.   *Reproduced from the original photograph by Nancy Powell, Fort Sheridan*

West onto Whistler Road, a one-way street, is the south side of the tower complex and the area where the soldiers lived, worked and played. Stretching like rear guards for the tower complex stand Buildings **103, 104, 105, 106, 107** and **108**. These buildings were built between 1907 and 1908 from standardized plans of the Quartermaster General to serve as company kitchens for soldiers billeted in the tower complex. They were originally connected by covered passageways which were removed in 1922 and remodeled for offices in 1967. Of particular note about these otherwise unremarkable buildings is the way the lower part is strengthened to take the burden of the upper half — the footing and first several vertical feet of each building are wider than the foundation.

Building 106. *TASC, Fort Sheridan.*

Buildings 103-108 looking from East to West. *TASC, Fort Sheridan.*

Building 47, the original mess hall, designed by Holabird and Roche and built in 1891. "Mess Call" was a signal to stop whatever one was doing and move to the food, regardless of one's opinion of it.

TASC, Fort Sheridan.

The kitchens were purposely separated from the living and eating areas. This was a safety concern since kitchen fires were not an uncommon occurrence. Fort Sheridan not only had its separated kitchens and barracks but a separate dining facility.

Soldiers have traditionally accused mess sergeants of feeding them material fit for a scrap drive. An unusual mess sergeant who was assigned to the AATC (Anti-aircraft Artillery Training Center) at Fort Sheridan had actually thrived on his own diet of razor blades, nails, tacks, buttons, silver dollars and water glasses before joining the Army in 1941. His medical history revealed that in 1933 doctors gave this "All-American Chow Hound" with the cast-iron stomach only two years to live after he had swallowed a wrist watch. However, he defied the odds and became employed by Ringling Brothers, Barnum and Bailey.[72]

Building 47 also housed the central heating plant in a long side wing attached to the east side. Coal was brought to the plant and traveled through an underground tunnel to the boilers — another story for later. The only remaining evidence of the heating plant is the cut-back smokestack on the east side of the building. A greenhouse was also situated on this side and referred to as Building 47A. The wall still retains some markings of its location.

Building 47 has seen several other uses over the years. In the early 1900's it contained a post exchange, chapel, branch library, bowling alley, restaurant and a large hall used both as a gymnasium and for entertainment. During the second Officers' Training Camp (August 27-November 27, 1917), Marshall Field and Company, Chicago, maintained a Military Store in this building which sold uniforms and other equipment to the newly commissioned officers. At that time nothing was available from the Quartermaster. Each man had to purchase what he needed in the open market and within a week after graduation. The Fort Sheridan Association arranged volume buying, and Marshall Field and Company was able to provide a discount to alleviate the expense. (After World War I, Captain Marshall Field III became one of the Directors of the Fort Sheridan Association). Building 47 hosted such entertainers as the songstress Kate Smith and the Chicago Symphony Orchestra.[73] Later the building was used as a Post Exchange, Cafeteria, and Tailor Shop and has undergone further interior renovations to accommodate administrative offices.

Building 47.   *Reproduced from the original photograph by Nancy Powell, Fort Sheridan.*

Building 47.   *TASC, Fort Sheridan.*

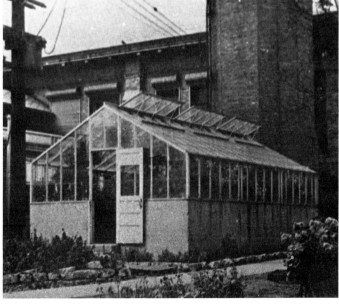

Building 47A. *Reproduced from the original photograph by Nancy Powell, Fort Sheridan.*

Off the path and southeast of Building 47 is Building **57A**, an innocuous looking structure that belies its function. It was built in 1892 and designed by Holabird and Roche for use as a Magazine, and it is still used for this purpose. Dynamite was stored in one of its two rooms, and the oak doors are sheathed with steel. This is the only building that has none of the brick detail which marks many Holabird and Roche designs at Fort Sheridan.

Building 57.

Reproduced from the original photograph by Nancy Powell, Fort Sheridan.

Building 57A.

The post Fire House, Building 79, is located on the south side of Whistler Road. It was built in 1893 and is one of the few buildings on post still serving its original utilitarian function.

This building is another Holabird and Roche design and was originally smaller but sufficient to accommodate horse-drawn apparatus. In 1927 a wood frame addition was added to the rear of the building to provide sleeping quarters, offices and a hose drying tower. In 1951 the wood structure was replaced with brick and a third bay added. At the same time the hose drying tower was replaced with a more modern air hose dryer. At some point, the original vehicular entrance was squared off and overhead doors replaced the sliding wood panelled doors. As part of the concern about fire and safety, the proximity of the Fire House to barracks, kitchens, heating plant and mess hall might be noted.

Building 79.

Fort Sheridan Museum.

Building 79.   *Reproduced from the original photograph by Nancy Powell, Fort Sheridan.*

Building 79.   *TASC, Fort Sheridan.*

Past the Fire House stands Building **60**, designed by Holabird and Roche and built in 1893 as an equestrian drill hall. The original arena measured 24,732 square feet and was used for drilling soldiers in mounted and dismounted positions during inclement weather. Mirrors hung around the arena so the soldiers could check their horses and horsemanship.

In 1946 the building was redesignated as a sports area which added a stage, hardwood floors and various partitions around the interior. The wrought iron rampart and door were replaced with the present wood doors and much of the original doorway bricked up. More recently, the sports arena was redesignated the post Fieldhouse, housing all the equipment associated with a modern gymnasium and offering soldiers an opportunity to maintain their ability to pass a required physical fitness test twice a year.

Building 60.   *Fort Sheridan Museum.*

Building 60.   *TASC, Fort Sheridan.*

Equestrian Drill Hall.　　　　　　　　　　　　　　　　　　*Fort Sheridan Museum.*

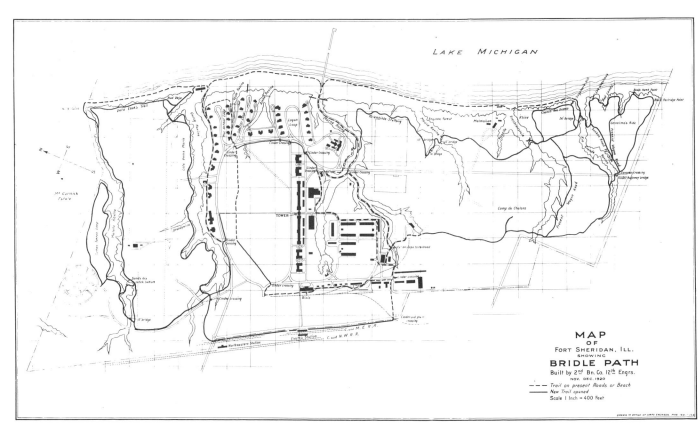

Fort Sheridan Museum.

Farther west on Whistler Road stands Building **66**, originally designed by the post engineer as a Post Office. The Post Office remained so from 1907, when it was built, until 1941 when it was remodeled for use as a Chaplains' School, and at another time as the post's nursery and the Reenlistment Office. An addition was built in 1917.

The Post Office served Fort Sheridan well, but its revenue depended on the number of people stationed on the post which fluctuated from year to year. The first postmistress, appointed on December 1, 1910, was Jennie DeRoo, one of the first female post office officials in the United States.[74] It now serves as administrative offices.

Building 66.

Reproduced from the original photograph by Nancy Powell, Fort Sheridan.

Building 66.

TASC, Fort Sheridan.

At the end of Whistler Road is Building **33**. (During World War II it was known as Hotel 33). It was designed by Holabird and Roche and built in 1890 as a stockade to accommodate 72 prisoners whose offenses ranged from drunkenness to attempted desertion. The two long, flanking wings were also designed by Holabird and Roche and added in 1905 and 1906, bringing the total capacity to 120 prisoners.

The south wing accommodates a Law Enforcement Agency office, and the central block and north wing house the Fort Sheridan Museum. Four cell blocks remain in place, two in the south wing and two in the central block. They are constructed of interlaced steel bands on four sides, much like a box. In addition, eight solitary confinement cells on the main level of the central block and six in the basement of the north wing remain in place.

The keys and locks were made by Folger Adams of Joliet, Illinois, using prison labor. They were controlled by a mechanism known as gang lock: A lever in a metal box in the passageway outside the cell block could open or lock all the doors simultaneously in case of emergencies.

The first level of the north wing once had a chapel, mess hall, kitchen and pantry. Stamped tin ceilings still remain in some of the rooms, as well as painted lines on the cell block floors of the central block which were used by prisoners lining up for inspection.

The Museum was established in 1957 by the Post Commander, Colonel John Hammond. It was located in Building 50 until 1968 when the museum closed pending location of better facilities. Then, for a very short time, it was in the basement of Building 84, where it might still be today if General Sheridan's carriage could have been accommodated. The carriage, which is on display at the museum, was found in a loft of one of the old stables. It is believed that General Sheridan rode in it during his last review of troops at Fort Sheridan on May 5, 1888. The central block and north wing have served as the Post Museum since 1970.

"Gang Lock."   *TASC, Fort Sheridan.*

Building 33. "The Guard House." Changing Guard. *Fort Sheridan Museum.*

Building 33 with a view of the north wing. *Fort Sheridan Museum.*

62

South onto Lyster Road (along the west side of the historic district) are two sets of quarters which are mirror images of each other. Buildings **90** and **91** were built in 1893 and designed by Holabird and Roche as two-family non-commissioned officers' quarters and remain so. However, when the need arose, these as well as other buildings on Lyster Avenue have been used as officers' quarters.

While there is nothing on record, the placement of the buildings suggests they were originally built to accommodate the non-commissioned officer in charge of the post stockade. A similar set of quarters, Building 59, also on the west side of Lyster Road, may have been used by the ordnance sergeant to place him close to his working area. These are two examples of the Army's interest in combining living and working areas.

Building **59** was built in 1892 and designed by Holabird and Roche as an Ordnance Storehouse. The first floor was divided into three rooms, and the basement was divided into two storage areas. The rooms on the south and north sides of the buildings were loading rooms for munitions and had outside entrances. The central room, the domain of the Ordnance Sergeant, had no outside entrance. In 1933 this building was converted to non-commissioned officers' quarters.

The role of ordnance has changed over the past several years. From its original mission of making and fusing munitions, the Ordnance Corps has become responsible for controlling explosive devices. This particular branch also provides pertinent instruction to local law enforcement agencies and public safety organizations as well as training for disaster response teams.

Immediately south of Building 59 is what used to be the post bakery, built in 1890 and designed by the architectural firm of Holabird and Roche. Two brick additions were constructed in 1919, one to the north side and one to the rear of the building. Two Marshall ovens, declared at the time as a "much improved oven," replaced the original brick ovens and were installed in 1919 and 1920. Building **34** served as a bakery from 1890 to 1940 and was then remodeled to serve as a Non-commissioned Officers Club until 1956. From 1956 to 1967 the post library was located here, and in 1967 the building began its current career as a child care center.

Still on the west side of Lyster Road and adjacent to Building 34 are Buildings **45** and **102.** They were built in 1910 from standardized plans of the Quartermaster General to house the non-commissioned officers assigned to Lovell General Hospital. They still serve as quarters for non-commissioned officers.

Building 90.

Building 34.

63

Building 59.

ASC, Fort Sheridan.   Building 45.   *Reproduced from the original photograph by Nancy Powell, Fort Sheridan.*

Building 45, which is architecturally identical to Building 102.

Building 46.

Building 140.

Nancy Powell, Fort Sheridan.

Building 88.

At the corner of Ronan and Lyster Roads is Building **46**, which is identical in design to Building **52** (Exchange Road) and Building 30 (Leonard Wood Avenue and McCaskey Road), all built between 1890 and 1891. These three buildings show none of the architectural influence which marks the other Holabird and Roche structures on the installation. They do, however, reflect the bungalow style which was predominant in the early part of the twentieth century. They originally housed non-commissioned officers but now serve as officers' quarters.

On the south side of Ronan Road and across the road from Building 46 stands Post Headquarters, Building 140. The Post Commander, a position roughly equivalent to a city mayor and city manager, and his staff, similar to a city council, manage the Fort Sheridan community from here.

This relatively new building is not considered of historic significance within the boundaries of the historic district. It was built in 1939 by the Stearnes Company of Chicago as the Bakers and Cooks School. However, besides instructing the culinary apprentices, the Bakers and Cooks School made its own chapter in history by being one of the forerunners in perfecting the art of dehydrating food. A Bakers and Cooks School was established at Fort Sheridan in 1921 and was then housed in Building 82.

(There is an architectural similarity between this building and Building 142, located on Patten Road and built in 1939 by the Stearnes Company as non-commissioned officers' quarters.)

North of Building 140 is Building **88**, a small building relatively easy to miss among the larger structures on the post but part of the ordnance complex. It was designed by Holabird and Roche and built in 1893 as an Ordnance Storehouse for up to 10,000 gallons of oil. The oil has been removed, but the building continues to function as a storehouse for the installation.

Between Ronan and Thorpe Roads are Buildings **72, 78** and **44** respectively. These three buildings were built in 1892 and designed by Holabird and Roche as housing for stable sergeants and saddlers.

Again, here is a good example of how the soldier lived close to his work. The horses and mules that carried many of the post's soldiers and almost all their heavy equipment were entrusted to the stable sergeants, while the saddlers learned their trade at the Army Saddlers' School, Fort Riley, Kansas.

These buildings cannot be classified as a particular architectural style, although they seem to resemble the bungalow style already described. Buildings **72, 78** and **44** still function as housing for non-commissioned officers and enlisted personnel.

Not all the animals charged to the care of the stable sergeant were the impressive Cavalry mounts. The Army used a variety of mules for various jobs, each having its own number, name and function. One of the lesser known of these mules was Little Jimmy.

Little Jimmy was imported from France in 1918 to relieve a prisoner detail of hauling coal on a narrow gauge railroad winding through an underground tunnel beneath Building 47. Jimmy soon became wise to his labor and the necessary stops on his own private underground railway. When the loaders whistled, he would stop at the loading shaft to take on coal for the boilers, but on the return trip to reload Jimmy went non-stop past the coal shaft.

Building 72. *Reproduced from the original photograph by Nancy Powell, Fort Sheridan.*

Time began to take its toll on Jimmy. The overhead in the tunnel was low and sloping and began to wear down his ears. Several remedies were attempted to prevent the continual chafing, including tying his ears down with a bandana, taping them to his head and wearing a specially designed hard hat. All met with failure until a kindly veterinarian performed minor surgery on Jimmy and, in the style of the times, bobbed his ears a few inches. Jimmy went about his coal hauling duties quietly and patiently until his death in 1923.[75] With Jimmy's demise and fewer prisoners in the cell blocks, the tunnel was closed and a ramp built on the west side of the building for trucks to unload the coal for the boilers.

Almost across the road from Building 72 is Building 89. At first glance the building appears to be a carriage house, but Holabird and Roche designed it for a far different function. It was built in 1892 to house artillery pieces, the kind immortalized in the Army Song, "The Caissons Go Rolling Along," and used to transport heroes to their final resting place; instruments of war used for a more humane function. Building 89 could house a complete field artillery battery consisting of six artillery pieces.

In 1922 it was remodeled for use as a transportation garage, and again in 1940 it was remodeled as an ordnance machine and tin shop. Some time during these alterations, the large door on the south side of the building was added and the overhead door installed. It is now used as a storage warehouse.

Building 72.

Building 89.   *TASC, Fort Sheridan.*

Building 62.   *Reproduced from the original photograph by Nancy Powell, Fort Sheridan.*

69

On the south side of Ronan Road are Buildings **65, 62, 63, 42** and **43**, five of six stables designed by Holabird and Roche and built between 1890 and 1893. The hoist beams still seen on some of the buildings were used to lift baled hay to the lofts, and the dormers provided light to the loft area.

Buildings 42 and 43 were considered unusually elaborate for a utilitarian purpose and serve notice even now of the importance of the horses and mules owned by the Army at that time. The Officers' Manual, required of every newly commissioned officer, stated on the inside front cover (circa 1930) that an officer "cared for his soldiers and his horse before caring for himself." While the equipment is vastly different, the principle remains a paramount consideration.

Within the stable area, now used for the Main Exchange, Quartermaster repair shops, warehouses and administration, one might reflect on the training horses and mules received. It was strict, as strict as any training their mounted counterparts received. Horses assigned to the Field Artillery were trained to stand rock steady when the cannons were being fired. Cavalry horses were trained to stand and move during exchanges of small arms ammunition, often at their own peril. If necessary, the final command a horse responded to was to lie down, so the mounted soldier could use his horse as a hasty barrier. It was a command from which the mounts seldom recovered. One of the drill regulations during the World War I era of horse-drawn artillery was: "Speak gently and never lose your temper" — while the Captain profanely tells you his state of mind![76]

The animals were acquired by the Quartermaster Corps from relay stations in Kansas, Nebraska and Missouri, the latter producing the prime mules. The mules were used to pull vehicles and carry pack loads and learned by example after two months' training alongside an experienced mule. The stables were arranged in a block pattern with the buildings and corrals forming portions of the fenced exercise yard. Each stable had its own stable sergeant who was responsible for the care and branding of his charges.

Horses were used on the post as late as 1941 and were briefly reinstated as a war-time measure during World War II. However, this experiment was not successful since trained Cavalry horses did not readily adjust to pulling wagons. Mules were increasingly hard to obtain, and qualified teamsters were scarce.[77]

Training On The Beach

Fort Sheridan Museum

Building 43. *Reproduced from the original photograph by Nancy Powell, Fort Sheridan.*

In the practice of maintaining form and function within relatively close confines, Building **39**, on the south side of Thorpe Road, was located close to the stable area. It was built in 1891 and designed by Holabird and Roche as a forage warehouse, a granary.

Aside from the additional doors on the north side and a concrete loading platform on the south side added in 1934, the building remains much as it was when built and is a notable example of warehouse architecture. The building still serves as a warehouse and deserves some examination. It has three floors, the first supported by massive stone and brick piers in the basement. The second floor is constructed of 2″ by 7½″ boards set on edge, making the flooring 7½″ thick. There is basically one large room on each floor with a brick structure housing an elevator located in the center of the building and still intact. It was not heated until 1929.

An unused portion of Building 39 was the training site for the first bicycle detachment in the United States Army. The detachment was part of the 15th Infantry Regiment assigned to Fort Sheridan and was under the command of Lieutenant Henry J. Hunt. Its purpose was to test the feasibility of bicycle riding as a sort of pedaled cavalry.

The detachment consisted of ten men who completed their debut ride in 1892: 14.75 miles in one hour and twenty-five minutes. Each rider carried his weapon and thirty-seven pounds of equipment. When some of his contemporaries poked fun at his unusual ensemble, Lieutenant Hunt quickly pointed out that Infantry soldiers similarly equipped would have taken at least five hours to complete the same trip.[78]

The first bicycle detachment pedaled its way into the history of military attempts to increase the efficiency of its soldiers as the Army gave way to the age of mechanization.

Adjacent and south of Building 39 stands Building 119, built in 1913 by the Quartermaster General, United States Army. This building was originally a non-commissioned officers' quarters and then remodeled in 1921 for offices. When Fifth United States Army was in residence, their film library was located here. The offices are now used for administrative purposes. Building 119 is one of the background buildings within the boundaries of the historic district. (Post Headquarters and the theater are the other two).

Building **77** is located north of Buildings 39 and 119. It was designed by Holabird and Roche and built in 1892. Originally, the building was used as a blacksmith shop and had five chimneys on the west wall; two remain intact but are not used. However, its utility as a modern-day blacksmith shop provides maintenance for the Transportation Motor Pool.

All of the buildings in the historic district have undergone interior renovations in keeping up with modernization, and very few relics were overlooked. Building 77 once had a skylight which the blacksmith would open to obtain relief from the heat of his forge. The metal lever that controlled the skylight is one of those relics and remains in place even though the skylight has disappeared.

Building 39.

Building 119.

Nancy Powell, Fort Sheridan.

Building 77.   *Reproduced from the original photograph by Nancy Powell, Fort Sheridan.*

Building 77.   *TASC, Fort Sheridan.*

Near the intersection of Thorpe and Lyster Roads stands Building 35, currently used as administrative offices for hiring, training, promoting and retiring the civilian employees working on Fort Sheridan. Originally, Building 35 served a different purpose. It was designed by Holabird and Roche and built in 1890 as quartermaster and commissary storehouses.

The interior was remodeled in the late 1950's, and the building was converted to a Non-commissioned Officers' Club. It was again remodeled in the middle 1960's for its present use.

It is interesting to note that this building and its companion, Building 100, were built farther away from the soldiers they served than was the forage warehouse, an equivalent building for the horses and mules.

Building 35.

TASC, Fort Sheridan.

Building 35.

Building **100**, the original cold storage house constructed in 1897, stands directly behind Building 35. The architect is unknown, but the building bears some of Holabird and Roche's distinctive characteristics. It was originally part of the quartermaster and commissary storehouses and stored up to forty quarters of beef at a time. The original plans called for six windows. All except the one above the door has been infilled with brick and, in some cases, covered with cement. The concrete loading platform was constructed on the south and east sides in 1932. This structure serves no visible function today and appears to be the post's only orphan within the historic district.

South of Building 100 and on the west side of Lyster Road is Building **36**, built in 1890 and designed by Holabird and Roche as a workshop. Six rounded arched entrances once provided access to six different shops and are just the right height for loading and unloading wagons. At some unrecorded date, a seventh entrance was constructed from one of the windows to provide an entrance for a seventh shop. Building 36 contained a shop for the blacksmith, pointer, plumber, saddler, carpenter, wheelwright, and had a storeroom for stones. During the occupation of the post by Lovell General Hospital (1918-1920) a switchboard panel was added in Building 36 to take care of the extra workload. This building has survived further renovation and is now used as a warehouse.

Behind Building 36 is Building **85**, built in 1905 from standardized plans provided by the Quartermaster General. This building was first used as a Quartermaster warehouse and is still part of the Quartermaster system as the installation's Clothing Sales Store. An Executive Order published July 1, 1950, authorized a cash clothing allowance system which provided a monthly cash allowance for soldiers to buy their clothes. This allowance began the seventh month of service, and the first fitting was done at the government's expense. Women's clothing was somewhat harder to obtain and had to be ordered from the Quartermaster Depot at Fort Leavenworth, Kansas.

Building 100.

Building 85.

Building 36.   *TASC, Fort Sheridan.*

Building 85.   *TASC, Fort Sheridan.*

Building 61.   *Reproduced from the original photograph by Nancy Powell, Fort Sheridan.*   **Building 61.**

Building 38.   *Fort Sheridan Museum.*   **Building 38.**

TASC, Fort Sheridan.

Slightly south of Building 85 is Building **61**, the post's Veterinary Clinic. It was built in 1910 from standardized plans of the Quartermaster General as a blacksmith shop, remodeled in 1936 for an ordnance machine shop, and in 1959 it was converted to its present use.

Huddled in the same complex as Building 85 is Building **38**, constructed in 1890 from plans by Holabird and Roche. This is a curious building, for the bronze plaque on the northeast corner reads: "Originally constructed as a Veterinarian Hospital, 1890." However, records indicate the building's original purpose was Quartermaster stables. Its form differs markedly from that of other stables on the installation, and it may have been intended as a veterinary hospital from the beginning.

There is a brick wall twelve inches thick which separates the Post Office (facing East), the Military Police Station (facing West), and commissary offices (facing North). The loft is still in its original condition and holds two oat bins over the rear wing of the building. Two projecting gables on the facade and rear wings were once loft doors but have been infilled with brick. In 1969 a concrete loading dock was added which facilitated the rededication of the building as a post office.

In 1918, when Lovell General Hospital was being constructed, Building 38 housed the constructing quartermaster and the contractor. After construction was completed, it was remodeled as barracks for the hospital staff. In 1945 this particular facility provided a branch post exchange and cafeteria for the convenience of the soldiers.

Directly across the road from Building 38 stands Building **37**, built in 1892 from plans provided by Holabird and Roche.

It was originally constructed as quarters for the stable guard and now serves as non-commissioned officers' quarters.

The completion of the stable complex begins with Building **80**, south of Building 37 and on the west side of Lyster Road. It was built between 1892 and 1893 and designed by Holabird and Roche.

Immediately south of Building 80 are two more former stables. Buildings **86** and **98** were built between 1909 and 1910 from standardized plans of the Quartermaster General, and all three of these buildings were designed as Quartermaster stables. At one time there was a wagon shed conveniently located directly across the road from this cluster of stables. These buildings are now used as warehouses.

Building 37.   *Fort Sheridan Museum.*

Building 37.

Building 80. *Reproduced from the original photograph by Nancy Powell, Fort Sheridan.*

Building 98. *TASC, Fort Sheridan.*

Up to now this tour has dealt with the enlisted soldiers and non-commissioned officers, where they worked and lived. North toward the flagpole and east onto Leonard Wood Avenue is the residential area of the officers. At the intersection of Westover and Lyster Roads is another relatively new structure considered a background building within the confines of the historic district. Building 180 has always been a theater and was constructed in 1932 by the Quartermaster General.

The first building on the north side of Leonard Wood Avenue is Building 32, Sheridan House. This two-story brick structure was built between 1907 and 1908 from the standardized plans of the Quartermaster General for bachelor officers' quarters. In 1922 the building was remodeled as a guest house and still serves that function for distinguished visitors to Fort Sheridan.

Building 180.   *Nancy Powell, Fort Sheridan.*

Building 32.   *TASC, Fort Sheridan*

East of Building 32 is Building **31**, designed by Holabird and Roche as two distinct sections and constructed in 1892. The western section was the officers' open mess and now serves the post as a community club (Sheridan Club). In 1954 a single story addition was attached and included the "Ratskeller." The eastern section was divided into twelve bachelor officers' quarters and now supplements the guest quarters.

Originally, the building was a long, rectangular 2½ story structure with a projecting wing on the facade and four projecting wings on the rear. Fire destroyed part of the western section in 1954 including the projecting wing on the front, or south side. The wing was rebuilt with a window above the main entrance. Below the window is a relief of General Sheridan on his horse. This crest is often used as the unofficial insignia of the post and was the idea of Colonel Benjamin O. Chapla, the post commander from 1962 to 1966. It was executed by his daughter with some assistance from the post's visual aids department. The mold is implanted at the front entrance of Sheridan House.

When Building 31 was a bachelor officers' quarters, each officer was assigned two rooms with closet and a bath. The Quartermaster furnished a mahogany round dining table, six chairs, two arm chairs, a desk with chair, a bookcase and an iron bed. Meals were available at $1.10 per day.

One of the early occupants was Second Lieutenant George S. Patton, Jr. On at least one occasion he described the food as "fierce," and added further that "the stuff on the table is not silver and not always clean and the service is punk." "I am the only man who dresses for dinner regularly and one of the few who wears a white collar and cuffs with my service clothes."[79]

Former employees of this building and a psychic have reported and unearthly presence in the El Morocco Lounge, the linen closet, and the basement. Apparently she is dressed in an orange-colored dress, resembles Mamie Eisenhower, and is very consciencious about her catering tasks. One can only surmise that the spirits of the past will live on, so to speak, enriching the post with their presence and tales of what might have been!

Fort Sheridan Museum.

Building 31. Quarters and Mess of the Bachelor Officers.   *Fort Sheridan Museum.*   Building 92.

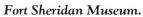

Building 29.

Building 31 with a view of the oriel window above the main entrance.

TASC, Fort Sheridan.

East from Building 31 is Building **97**, one of four two-family homes designed as Lieutenants' quarters in 1905 and constructed from the Quartermaster General's standardized plans. Buildings **92, 95** and **96** loop around Leonard Wood Avenue, and all four still provide housing for officers assigned to Fort Sheridan.

Lieutenant Patton was assigned to Troop K, 15th Cavalry, his first assignment upon graduation from the United States Military Academy at West Point, New York, in 1909. He married Beatrice Ayer in the Spring of 1910, and they subsequently occupied Building 92 from July, 1910 until December, 1911. Lieutenant Patton referred to his home as ''Allerdice House,'' probably referring to its former occupants.

East and beyond 97 and 96 is Building **30**, located at the junction of McCaskey Road and Leonard Wood Avenue. This is one of the three bungalow houses described earlier and was first occupied by the post engineer and assistant engineer.

McCaskey Road intersects Nicholson Road. Out Nicholson Road to its eastern terminus Building **29** has been standing since 1890. It has been in continuous use since then as the pumping station for the installation.

Water is collected through two intake pipes extending some 3,700 feet into Lake Michigan, the water source for the post. Purified and fluoridated water is sent from the pumping station to a 300,000 gallon clear well adjacent to the plant. This filtering system was installed in the late 1960's. Prior to that time, three pressure filter tanks had been in continuous operation since 1911 and were the last of their kind operating in the Great Lakes area. Fort Sheridan uses approximately 650,000 gallons of water during a twenty-four hour peak period. The landmark water tower and a water tower at the south end of the post supplement the distribution process.

TASC, Fort Sheridan.

TASC, Fort Sheridan.

The brick work on Building 29 is noteworthy, another example of an elaborate utilitarian building and the care Holabird and Roche brought to their work in the historic district.

Holabird and Roche designed a total of thirty-one one-family homes which were built between 1890 and 1892. The homes designed as captains' quarters (numbers **75, 76, 10, 11, 12, 13, 18, 19, 20, 53, 54, 73** and **74**) are a larger version of lieutenants' quarters and are distinguishable by the short side wing that replaces the projected bay employed on the lieutenants' quarters. (The sun porch on Building 53 was added in the late 1940's).

These homes had servants' quarters which were usually located on the third floor. At one time officers were authorized enlisted personnel, strikers, to function as their aides; and their employer was responsible for paying them some remuneration over and above the salary paid by the Army. Their duties included such things as keeping track of the officer's appointments, uniforms, and tack for the horses. The striker has gone the way of the horse, and the servants' quarters are more often used to give a teenager an extra measure of privacy.

A Captain's quarters.
TASC, Fort Sheridan.

The homes designed as lieutenants' quarters (numbers **3, 4, 5, 6, 7, 15, 16, 17, 21, 22, 23, 24, 25, 26, 27** and **56**) are representative of the Richardsonian Romanesque influence in architecture which was popular at the turn of the century and used by Holabird and Roche in both the living and working areas, except for the two post commandants' quarters. These and other buildings within the historic district have endured nearly one hundred years, even though they were given an expected life span of only thirty years.

In 1941, Victorian policies were set aside and a powder room was built from an existing closet on the first floor in most of the quarters. Yellow pine was used to form the treads of the stairs with much of the rest of the homes being floored with maple. Some Quartermaster furniture was available: it was made by Drexel, Duncan Phyfe design. Most of the kitchens have an attached butler's pantry, which, for the most part, has been converted for the convenience of the distaff side of the modern military family.

A Lieutenant's quarters.

All the homes weaving throughout the three loops show the distinctive features of either the original architects or the Army's standardized architectural plans. Other than the two commandants' homes, another exception is Building **28**, at the eastern end of MacArthur Loop. It was built in 1905, and the Quartermaster General designated this house for a field grade officer (Major through Colonel). It is now assigned to a General officer.

The two commandants' quarters are on Logan Loop, and en route there are two more buildings on Leonard Wood Avenue similar to numbers 92, 95, 96, and 97. Buildings **93** and **94** were constructed in 1905 as captains' quarters and designed from plans provided by the Quartermaster General. These two-family houses are larger than the lieutenants' quarters, and the porch wraps around the sides rather than the facade. There are also two rounded brick windows rather than a blind window in the gable end facade.

Continuing south, Leonard Wood Avenue intersects Scott Loop, where another ethereal resident of the post made his presence known December, 1977. Was he a resident of the old isolation hospital? Perhaps his bare head and long coat indicate he was a man of the cloth on a mission of mercy; after all, it was Christmas time. Or maybe he was a recalcitrant striker.

Building 28.

A Captain's quarters.

TASC, Fort Sheridan

87

Scott Loop illuminated with candles in bagged sand. A succession of three photographs revealed the above image.
Eric Lundahl, "Mr. Fotographer," TASC, Fort Sheridan.

Building 8, at the southeast corner of Logan Loop, was constructed in 1890 for the Post Commandant or a General officer. This, and its companion set of quarters, Building 9, are still considered unusually elegant and luxurious for military housing. During World War I, the interior was modified to accommodate part of the staff of Lovell General Hospital. The building was again modified in 1951 to accommodate two families. Of particular note about the exterior is the way Holabird and Roche set this and its companion off from the other buildings on the installation. They were designated for special people, and the firm felt they should look as special as their inhabitants by allowing the Queen Anne architecture to prevail.

Building 8.

Fort Sheridan Museum.

Building 9 was also built in 1890, and its grandeur was eloquently described in **The Chicago Tribune**, January, 1889: "The Secretary of War has approved the plans for the building of Fort Sheridan military post at Highwood. It will be the most elaborate military post in the United States, if indeed the entire world. The post will be dominated by a most luxurious commandant's mansion, fitted with every ingenious contrivance to be had . . ."

Building 9.

TASC, Fort Sheridan.

. . . AND FADE AWAY?

In times past, Fort Sheridan's fate could be compared to an old soldier — "retire" the post, and let it fade away.

Not long after the second Civilian Military Training Camp ended (November 17, 1917), the Navy cast an envious eye upon the reservation. Their plan was to establish a training school for Merchant Marine officers with Navy enlisted men as candidates; and Captain W. A. Moffett, then Commandant of Great Lakes Naval Training Station, would assume control. The instigators of this plan refused to divulge their names to Chicago newspapermen: "If we can put it over and get Fort Sheridan, we will be pleased to get publicity, for it will be a great accomplishment. But if we fail, we do not want to be known." They are still unknown.[80]

In 1932 there was consideration of closing Fort Sheridan when the liquidation of twelve Army posts was ordered by President Herbert Hoover in the interest of national economy. There was a sigh of relief when the headline "Fort Sheridan Not Included in Disbandment" was published. But in September, 1933, the fear was revived when President Franklin D. Roosevelt considered the evacuation of fifty more garrisons. Fort Sheridan once again escaped the axe![81]

The question of its fate was revived in June, 1971, when Fifth Army left its headquarters at Fort Sheridan and moved to Fort Sam Houston, Texas. It was during this time that some politicians became intent on obtaining recreational use of the post. At one point, the Illinois Department of Conservation submitted a plan to President Richard Nixon to turn over 170 acres to the State of Illinois. The Army was unwilling to cede ownership of any portion of its land.[82]

Once again, in 1978, Fort Sheridan was on the United States Department of Defense list of approximately eighty-five military installations to be studied for possible realignment and consolidation. Senator Adlai Stevenson (Democrat, Illinois) probably best summed it up by saying:

(Fort Sheridan is) ". . . grossly underutilized and contains almost seven-hundred acres of land with two miles of beachfront, in the most park-starved metropolitan area in the country."[83]

Plans to move the Military Enlistment Processing Command (MEPCOM) to Great Lakes in 1980 caused some trepidation in the community. A group of concerned Lake County citizens banded together and formed an organization known as Save Our Base. These were citizens who feared the probable economic impact of such a move within the community and were supported by Save Our Sheridan, a post-based organization. Save Our Base was a sub-committee of the Lake County Economics Development Commission.[84] The lobbyists went to work, and the post was saved.

In these intervening years, Fort Sheridan has also been considered for: a minimum security prison, a college, a mental institution, a forest preserve, a national military cemetery, and a residential development. Finally, on May 2, 1979, the City Council of the City of Chicago adopted a resolution that in essence recognized the significance of the post "for security and other purposes" and that its "fading away" would not be in the best interest of Chicago. The resolution is signed by former Mayor Jane Byrne and hangs in the Fort Sheridan Museum. It would seem that the permanence of Fort Sheridan was destined when General Henry Dearborn advocated a "strong stockade at Chikago with a view to establishment of a Post."[85]

Like the interminable Lake Michigan waves buffeting the beach, Fort Sheridan will probably always remain under scrutiny. Regardless of its fate, there can be no ending to Fort Sheridan's legacy until "Taps," — and soldiers will no longer continue to be a part of the View From The Tower.

"Taps"

Mike Orrico, Sparta, Wisconsin

ROADWAYS OF FORT SHERIDAN

BOLLES LOOP. Named for Brigadier General Frank C. Bolles, who assumed command of Fort Sheridan August, 1931. The housing area was constructed in 1967.

BRADLEY LOOP. Named for Major Alfred E. Bradley, Medical Corps Surgeon from 1906 to 1907.

BROWN STREET. Named for Colonel Edward T. Brown, who assumed command of Fort Sheridan August, 1910.

BULLOCK DRIVE. Named for Colonel Stephen E. Bullock, who assumed command of Fort Sheridan July, 1951. The housing area was constructed between 1956 and 1957.

BURKHARDT ROAD. Named for Colonel Samuel Burkhardt, Jr., who assumed command of Fort Sheridan December, 1917.

CHAPMAN ROAD. Named for Lieutenant Colonel L. A. T. Chapman, who assumed temporary command of Fort Sheridan July, 1918.

CHATFIELD COURT. Named for Major Walter H. Chatfield, who assumed temporary command of Fort Sheridan on four different occasions between 1906 and 1912. The housing area was constructed in 1967.

DAVIS COURT. Named for Master Sergeant Fred W. Davis, former Post Sergeant Major and veteran of World War I.

FINLEY ROAD. Named for Lieutenant Colonel Walter L. Finley, who assumed command of Fort Sheridan July, 1907.

FORBES ROAD. Named for Lieutenant Colonel Theodore F. Forbes, who assumed command of Fort Sheridan October, 1901.

GEORGE BELL ROAD. See Patten Road.

GORDON JOHNSTON DRIVE. Named for Colonel Gordon Johnston, a distinguished American soldier. The housing project, including Davis Court, was constructed between 1966 and 1967.

LEONARD WOOD AVENUE. Named for Major General Leonard Wood, Commander, Department of the East between 1910 and 1914.

LOGAN LOOP. Named for General John A. Logan, distinguished American soldier and national citizen of Illinois who took part in the War Between the States.

LYSTER ROAD. Named for Major William J. Lyster, the first Commanding Officer of Fort Sheridan.

MacARTHUR LOOP. Named for Lieutenant General Arthur MacArthur, a distinguished American soldier during the Spanish American War and the Philippine Insurrection, and father of General Douglas A. MacArthur.

MACOMB ROAD. Named for Major Augustus C. Macomb, who assumed command of Fort Sheridan October, 1906. (Macomb Road runs West to East, perpendicular to Bolles Loop).

In 1948, this area encompassed the Fort Sheridan Trailer Camp. The camp was designed for non-commissioned officers and had a capacity of 190 residents. It was patterned after a small city with its own mayor and three aldermen. The conveniences included laundry and telephone rooms, storage area, mail delivery and men's and women's wash rooms. The trailers were parked on concrete blocks that were once used as tent sites.[86] The building on the south side of the roadway was constructed in 1936 to serve as a meeting place for the Fort Sheridan Boy Scout troop. All of the materials were donated by a committee of North Shore businessmen.[87]

McCASKEY ROAD. Named for Colonel William S. McCaskey, who assumed command of Fort Sheridan March, 1902.

McCORMICK DRIVE. Named for Colonel Robert R. McCormick, 61st Coast Artillery Commander, Fort Sheridan, September, 1918, and former owner and publisher of the CHICAGO TRIBUNE.

McKIBBIN ROAD. Named for Captain Chambers McKibbin, who assumed temporary command of Fort Sheridan December, 1890.

NICHOLSON ROAD. Named for Colonel William J. Nicholson, who assumed command of Fort Sheridan March, 1915. Groundbreaking for the Wherry housing project along Nicholson Road began in 1954. Senator Kenneth Spicer Wherry (Republican-Nebraska) was instrumental in passing Public Law #211 in 1949 to relieve the post-war housing shortage.

The Wherry Housing project provided for a private corporation to construct the homes and lease them to the government. The contract called for a seventy-five year lease, but the government bought the lease rights in 1963.

NORMAN HECK COURT. Named for Captain Norman W. Heck, former Commanding Officer, 204th Military Police Company, Fort Sheridan. The housing project was constructed in 1967.

PATTEN ROAD. This section of roadway was formerly Sheridan Road and was later named for Mrs. James A. Patten, a former resident of Evanston, Illinois. In 1929, Mrs. Patten donated the funds to build the south gate of the post as well as an athletic field which is located east of McKibbin Road. The only indication of the latter's former use is the score board that still looks over the field where teams from the Civilian Military Training Camps once competed.

PATTEN GATE: Inscription on the left plaque reads: FORT SHERIDAN U.S. MILITARY RESERVATION.

The inscription on the right plaque reads: GATES PRESENTED BY MRS. JAMES A. PATTEN OF EVANSTON, ILLINOIS AS A TOKEN TO GOOD CITIZENSHIP EXEMPLIFIED BY THE CIVILIAN MILITARY TRAINING CAMPS. ERECTED A.D. 1932.

In 1967 plans were made to install new brick piers, but these plans did not include remounting the plaques.

The Sheridan Road Bill honoring General Sheridan was passed by the Illinois Legislature in 1895, and eventually a first-class carriage road was established between Chicago, Milwaukee and Green Bay.[88]

In the course of its route northward, Sheridan Road bisected the post, passed through the sally port of the water tower and skirted the parade field on the west side.

Sheridan Road coincided with historians' version of the old Green Bay Trail as it crossed the rifle range and continued to the site of Sacred Heart Academy (now Woodlands Academy, Lake Forest) where it returned to its present route. This section of roadway is now known as George Bell Road, named for Major General George Bell, Jr., former Corps Area Commander and distinguished American soldier. George Bell Road terminates at the North Shore Memorial U.S. Army Reserve Center.

The original "South Gate."   *TASC, Ft. Sheridan.*

General Sheridan astride Rienzi at the outset of Sheridan Road, Lincoln Park, Chicago, Illinois.

Chicago Park District

North Shore Memorial USAR Center.

The rifle range is now referred to as Haley Army Heliport, named for Captain Patrick Haley, who was killed in action in Vietnam, 1967. The airfield was constructed in 1953 by troop labor.

It was near this site that the United States Cavalry was reactivated. On June 12, 1977, CBS Television Network and its correspondents, Dan Rather, Charles Kuralt and Barbara Howar, televised ON THE ROAD WITH CHARLES KURALT with Colonel C. Cosby Kerney, United States Army, retired, and the founder of the United States Cavalry Association Reactivated.

For a brief moment he and his troopers were able to relive the glory days of the Cavalry, renouncing the John Wayne image of the yellow neckerchief and flopping elbows and emphasizing the advantages of the horse over a half-track![89]

ROBINSON ROAD. Named for Major Frank U. Robinson, who assumed temporary command of Fort Sheridan April, 1903.

RONAN ROAD. Named for George Ronan, a civilian scout and prominent frontiersman connected with the Fort Dearborn Massacre.

SARGENT ROAD. Named for Major Fredrick H. Sargent, who assumed temporary command of Fort Sheridan July, 1913.

SCOTT LOOP. Named for General Winfield Scott, a distinguished American soldier and commander of the expedition sent from the east to take part in the Black Hawk War.

THORPE ROAD. Named for Captain Frank Thorpe, who assumed temporary command of Fort Sheridan May, 1899.

VATTMAN ROAD. Named for Major E.J. Vattman, Chaplain to the two Reserve Officer Training Camps at Fort Sheridan. He resided in Wilmette, Illinois, and retired at the age of sixty-four. Major Vattman is buried in the Post Cemetery.

WADE COURT. Named for Colonel Clearfield P. Wade, who assumed command of Fort Sheridan July, 1953.

WAINWRIGHT COURT. Named for General Jonathan M. Wainwright, distinguished American soldier and former resident of Fort Sheridan. While his father, Major R.P. Page Wainwright, was stationed at Fort Sheridan, General Wainwright graduated from Elm Place School, Highland Park, 1897.

The Jonathan Wainwright Underpass to Morgan Park playground at Sheridan Road and Elm Place was dedicated to him October, 1943.

The housing project was constructed between 1966 and 1967.

WESTOVER ROAD. To date, no record of the dedication of this road has been found.

WHISTLER ROAD. Named for Captain John Whistler, the first Commander of Fort Dearborn.

UNITS AND DATE OF ACTIVATION
AT FORT SHERIDAN

6th Infantry Regiment (Companies F and K)	1887
15th Infantry Regiment (2 battalions)	1891
1st Artillery Regiment (Light Gun Battery E)	1891
7th Cavalry (Troops B and K)	1892
4th Infantry Regiment	1896
6th Infantry Regiment	1896
5th Infantry Regiment (one battalion)	1900
7th Infantry Regiment	1900
3rd Cavalry (Troop B)	1900
5th Artillery (Light Gun Battery D)	1900
15th Cavalry (3rd Squadron)	1908
27th Infantry Regiment	1913
5th Cavalry	1916
40th Infantry	1917
149th Field Artillery	1917
112th Engineers	1917
61st Coast Artillery	1918
201st Coast Artillery	1920
14th Cavalry	1920
3rd Field Artillery	1920
2nd Infantry	1920
103rd Coast Artillery	1941
40th Anti-Aircraft Artillery Brigade	1941
29th WAAC (Womens Army Auxiliary Corps)	1942
45th Anti-Aircraft Brigade	1942
Army Service Forces 6th Service Command	1943
728th Military Police Battalion	1947
5012 ASU Escort Company	1947
5th United States Army Band	1949
204th Military Police Company	1952
5th Region United States Army Air Defense Command	1954
5th United States Army Flight Detachment	1959
5043 Transfer Company	1961
578th Ordnance Company	1962
543rd Explosive Ordnance Detachment	1962
Headquarters, Fifth United States Army	1967
202nd Military Police Company	1967
Headquarters, Detachment A, 5th Military Police Group	1970
United States Army Chicago District Recruiting Command (now known as United States Army Recruiting Battalion Chicago)	1971
CINA (Coordinating Element Northern Area)	1971
United States Army 5th Recruiting District	1971
Headquarters, 5th United States Army Veterinary Food Inspection Service	1971
United States Army Advisory Group	1971
United States Army Chief of Engineers Inspector General (Chicago Field Office)	1971
Headquarters, 45th Artillery Brigade	1971
30th Hospital Center	1972
525th Army Security Detachment	1972
81st Army Band	1972
85th Division Maneuver Training Command (MTC)	1973
Headquarters, United States Army Recruiting Command (USAREC)	1973
United States Army Midwest Regional Recruiting Command (now known as United States Army 4th Recruiting Brigade Midwest)	1973
United States Army Criminal Investigation Command	1973
112th Military Intelligence Command	1973
United States Army Readiness and Mobilization Region V (ARMR V)	1973
Headquarters, United States Army Readiness and Mobilization Flight Detachment	1973
United States Army Readiness Group Sheridan	1973
51st Explosive Ordnance Disposal (EOD)	1973
Headquarters, 28th Air Defense Artillery	1974
Untied States Army Communications Command	1974*
533rd Engineer Detachment	1974
902nd Military Intelligence Group	1974*
Military Enlistment Processing Command (MEPCOM)	1976
North Shore Memorial Reserve Center (425th Transportation Brigade Headquarters)	1976
Headquarters, 4th United States Army	1984

* - Approximate

NOTE: No source of information clearly identifies all the units that have been assigned to Fort Sheridan.

BIBLIOGRAPHY

1. NATURALIST IN THE GREAT LAKES REGION, Elliot R. Downing, The University of Chicago Press, 1922, pages 59-64.

2. Ibidem, page 1.

3. Ibidem, page 112.

4. Ibidem, page 64.

5. "Endangered and Threatened Species and/or Critical Habitat and Natural Areas of Fort Sheridan," Fort Sheridan, Illinois. Illinois Department of Conservation, September 11, 1978.

6. A HISTORY OF LAKE COUNTY ILLINOIS, John J. Halsey, 1912, Roy S. Bates, pages 281-282.

7. Ibidem, page 264.

8. Ibidem, page 267.

9. Ibidem, page 273.

10. HISTORY OF DEERFIELD, ILLINOIS, Marie Ward Reichelt, Glenview Press, 1928, page 8.

11. THE GREAT CHICAGO FIRE, Robert Cromie, McGraw Hill Book Company, Inc., New York, 1958, page 5.

12. HISTORY OF DEERFIELD, ILLINOIS, Marie Ward Reichelt, Glenview Press, 1928, page 136.

13. HOW IT ALL BEGAN, Joe Meads, page 19.

14. HISTORY OF DEERFIELD, ILLINOIS, Marie Ward Reichelt, Glenview Press, 1928, page 7.

15. HOW IT ALL BEGAN, Joe Meads, page 4.

16. 28 MILES NORTH, THE STORY OF HIGHWOOD, Marvyn Wittelle, Highwood History Foundation, Inc., 1953, pages 19-21. PIONEER TO COMMUTER, THE STORY OF HIGHLAND PARK, Marvyn Wittelle, the Rotary Club of Highland Park, Illinois, 1958, page 30.

17. THE LIFE OF GENERAL PHILIP H. SHERIDAN, F.A. Burr and R.J. Hinton, 1888, page 355. SHERIDAN THE INEVITABLE, Richard O'Connor, The Bobbs-Merrill Company, Inc., 1953, page 314.

18. THE LIFE OF GENERAL PHILIP H. SHERIDAN, F.A. Burr and R.J. Hinton, 1888, page 356.

19. THE GREAT CHICAGO FIRE, Robert Cromie, McGraw Hill Book Company, Inc., New York, 1958, page 275.

20. THE LIFE OF GENERAL PHILIP H. SHERIDAN, F.A. Burr and R.J. Hinton, 1888, pages 357-358.

21. CHICAGO, A PERSONAL HISTORY OF AMERICA'S MOST AMERICAN CITY, Finnis Farr, Arlington House, New Rochelle, New York, 1973, page 87.

22. CHICAGO HISTORY, THE MAGAZINE OF THE CHICAGO HISTORICAL SOCIETY, Spring, 1983. "Whose City?" Public and Private Places in Nineteenth-Century Chicago, Perry Duis, page 6.

23. A HISTORY OF LAKE COUNTY ILLINOIS, John J. Halsey, 1912, Roy S. Bates, page 197.

24. A HISTORY OF LAKE FOREST, ILLINOIS, Edward Arpee, 1964, page 121.

25. Fort Sheridan Museum file of United States Military Reservations, War Department, Washington, D.C., 1916, pages 114-122.

26. 28 MILES NORTH, THE STORY OF HIGHWOOD, Marvyn Wittelle, Highwood History Foundation, Inc., 1953, page 33.

27. CHICAGO HISTORY, THE MAGAZINE OF THE CHICAGO HISTORICAL SOCIETY, Spring, 1983. "Whose City?" Public and Private Places in Nineteenth-Century Chicago, Perry Duis, page 16.

28. THE LIFE OF GENERAL PHILIP H. SHERIDAN, F.A. Burr and R.J. Hinton, 1888. SHERIDAN THE INEVITABLE, Richard O'Connor, The Bobbs-Merrill Company, Inc., 1953.

29. FORTS OF THE WEST, Robert W. Frazer, University of Oklahoma Press, 1965, pages 39 and 187.

30. SHERIDAN THE INEVITABLE, Richard O'Connor, The Bobbs-Merrill Company, Inc., 1953, page 352.

31. Fort Sheridan Museum records of the diary of Albert Jacobs, one of the soldiers.

32. THE TOWER, November 4, 1983. Information obtained from National Archives, Washington, D.C.

33. Fort Sheridan Museum records.

34. 28 MILES NORTH, THE STORY OF HIGHWOOD, Marvyn Wittelle, Highwood History Foundation, Inc., 1953, page 26.

35. City Hall, Highwood, Illinois; interviews; Fort Sheridan Museum records; "The Forgotten Village," an unpublished account of Highwood, Ruth Rettig Reilly.

36. 28 MILES NORTH, THE STORY OF HIGHWOOD, Marvyn Wittelle, Highwood History Foundation, Inc., 1953.

37. City Hall, Highwood, Illinois.

38. NORTH SHORE LINE MEMORIES, George V. Campbell, Quality Books, Inc., Northbrook, Illinois, 1980, pages 28 and 31.

39. FORT SHERIDAN AT ATTENTION AND REST, H.G. Mackern, 1897. A real estate brochure on file at Newberry Library, Chicago, Illinois.

40. THE TOWER, August 26, 1983.

41. SITTING BULL AND THE INDIAN WARS, W. Fletcher Johnson, Edgewood Publishing Company, 1891.

42. THE FORT SHERIDAN ASSOCIATION, ITS HISTORY AND ACHIEVEMENTS, Myron E. Adams and Fred Girton, 1920, pages 174 and 175.

43. Ibidem, page 14.

44. Ibidem, page 18.

45. CHICAGO TRIBUNE, October 24, 1918.

46. HISTORY OF DEERFIELD, ILLINOIS, Marie Ward Reichelt, Glenview Press, 1928, page 57.

47. THE TOWER, September 22, 1950.

48. THE REVEILLE, November 16, 1917.

49. United States Army Construction Division Report, March 14, 1919.

50. Personal letter from Senator William Proxmire, December 16, 1983.

51. United States Army Construction Division Report, March 14, 1919.

52. THE TOWER, June 9, 1944.

53. CHICAGO DAILY TRIBUNE, October 26, 1922.

54. THE SHERIDAN, August 15, 1941.

55. THE TOWER, January 8, 1943.

56. THE TOWER, September 29, 1944.

57. THE TARGET, August 27, 1943.

58. THE TOWER, November 3, 1944.

59. THE TOWER, March 8, 1946.

60. THE TOWER, March 9, 1945.

61. "A German P.O.W. at Camp Grant, The Reminiscences of Heinz Richter," translated and edited by Anton H. Richter.

62. THE TOWER, April 13, 1951.

63. THE TOWER, April 27, 1951.

64. GUIDE TO THE MILITARY POSTS OF THE UNITED STATES, Francis Paul Prucha, S.J., The State Historical Society, Madison, Wisconsin, 1964.

65. Fort Sheridan Museum.

66. Historical American Buildings Survey, conducted by Sally Kress Tompkins, Real Property Office, Fort Sheridan. HIGHLAND PARK, AMERICAN SUBURB AT ITS BEST, Philip Berger.

67. Historical American Buildings Survey, conducted by Sally Kress Tompkins, Real Property Office, Fort Sheridan.

68. CHICAGO TRIBUNE, January 3, 1972.

69. "The History of Fort Sheridan, Illinois," prepared by Robert Schall, Second Lieutenant, The Clerical School and the Visual Aids Section, 1672nd Service Unit, January 1, 1944, pages 19 and 20.

70. A HISTORY OF LAKE FOREST, ILLINOIS, Edward Arpee, 1964, page 121.

71. THE TOWER, October 31, 1980.

72. THE TOWER, January 22, 1943.

73. THE REVEILLE, October 17, 1917. THE TARGET, March 26, 1943.

74. A HISTORY OF LAKE COUNTY, ILLINOIS, John J. Halsey, 1912, Roy S. Bates, page 578.

75. THE TOWER, August 18, 1944.

76. Diary of F.T. Edwards, page 84. On file at the Fort Sheridan Library.

77. THE TOWER, January 12, 1962.

78. "The Bearings," Chicago, June 3, 1892. Courtesy of Karl E. Wiegand.

79. THE PATTON PAPERS, Volume I, Martin Blumenson, Houghton Mifflin Company, 1972, pages 191-192.

80. "This History of Fort Sheridan, Illinois," prepared by Robert Schall, Second Lieutenant, The Clerical School and Visual Aids Section, 1672nd Service Unit, January 1, 1944, page 35.

81. Ibidem, page 54.

82. CHICAGO TRIBUNE, August 25, 1972.

83. SUBURBAN TRIBUNE, October 23, 1978.

84. CHICAGO TRIBUNE, December 3, 1980.

85. Encyclopedia Britannica.

86. THE WAUKEGAN NEWS-SUN, July 21, 1948.

87. THE FORT SHERIDAN NEWS, April 4, 1936.

88. "L.A.W. Bulletin and Good Roads," July 26, 1895, courtesy of Karl E. Wiegand.

89. CBS Television Network, Volume I, Broadcast 18, June 12, 1977.

NOTE: 1. Specific information regarding the buildings in the historic district was taken from "HABS Survey For Fort Sheridan, Illinois," conducted by Sally Kress Tompkins, Architectural Historian.

2. Specific information regarding roadways was obtained from Fort Sheridan General Orders #9, May 13, 1936; General Orders #111, December 23, 1969; and General Orders #110-27, June 3, 1985.

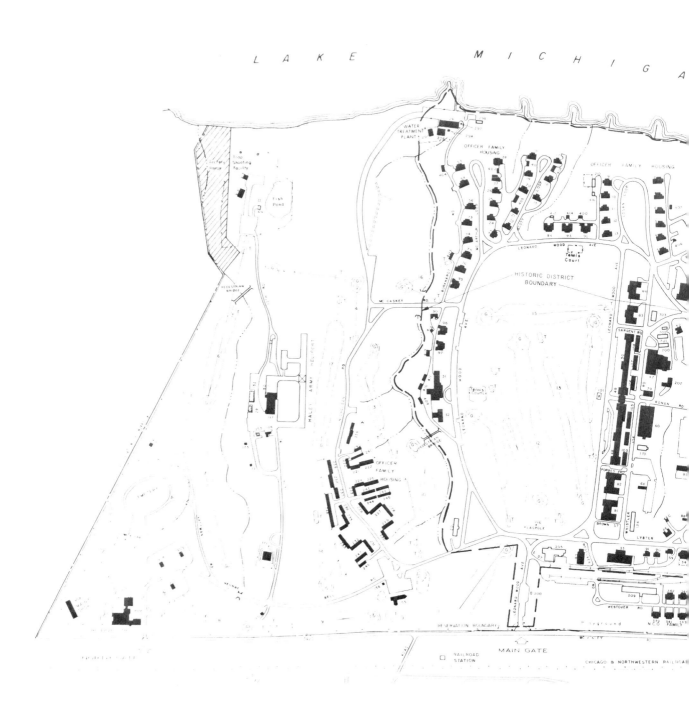

L A K E   M I C H I G A